The Clandestine Marriage ... By G. Colman and David Garrick ... A new edition.

George Colman, David Garrick

The BiblioLife Network

This project was made possible in part by the BiblioLife Network (BLN), a project aimed at addressing some of the huge challenges facing book preservationists around the world. The BLN includes libraries, library networks, archives, subject matter experts, online communities and library service providers. We believe every book ever published should be available as a high-quality print reproduction; printed on- demand anywhere in the world. This insures the ongoing accessibility of the content and helps generate sustainable revenue for the libraries and organizations that work to preserve these important materials.

The following book is in the "public domain" and represents an authentic reproduction of the text as printed by the original publisher. While we have attempted to accurately maintain the integrity of the original work, there are sometimes problems with the original book or micro-film from which the books were digitized. This can result in minor errors in reproduction. Possible imperfections include missing and blurred pages, poor pictures, markings and other reproduction issues beyond our control. Because this work is culturally important, we have made it available as part of our commitment to protecting, preserving, and promoting the world's literature.

GUIDE TO FOLD-OUTS, MAPS and OVERSIZED IMAGES

In an online database, page images do not need to conform to the size restrictions found in a printed book. When converting these images back into a printed bound book, the page sizes are standardized in ways that maintain the detail of the original. For large images, such as fold-out maps, the original page image is split into two or more pages.

Guidelines used to determine the split of oversize pages:

• Some images are split vertically; large images require vertical and horizontal splits.
• For horizontal splits, the content is split left to right.
• For vertical splits, the content is split from top to bottom.
• For both vertical and horizontal splits, the image is processed from top left to bottom right.

Clandestine Marriage.
New Edition. 1770.

Country Girl.
2d. Edition. 1767.

Neck or Nothing.
New Edition. 1774.

Cymon.
New Edit. 1773.

Peep behind the Curtain
1767.

Songs in the Jubilee. 1778.
and 1770.

King Arthur, a masque. 1770

THE

Clandeſtine Marriage,

A

COMEDY.

(Price One Shilling and Six-pence.)

THE

Clandeſtine Marriage,

A

COMEDY.

As it is ACTED at the

Theatre Royal in *Drury-Lane.*

BY

GEORGE COLMAN

AND

DAVID GARRICK.

Huc adhibe vultus, et in unâ parce duobus :
Vivat, et ejuſdem ſimus uterque parens !   OVID.

A NEW EDITION.

LONDON:
Printed for T. BECKET and P. A. DE HONDT, in the Strand.

M.DCC.LXX.

Advertisement.

HOGARTH's MARRIAGE-A-LA-MODE has before furnished Materials to the Author of a Novel, published some Years ago, under the Title of *The Marriage-Act*: But as that Writer pursued a very different Story, and as his Work was chiefly designed for a Political Satire, very little Use could be made of it for the Service of this Comedy.

In Justice to the Person, who has been considered as the sole Author, the Party, who has hitherto lain concealed, thinks it incumbent on him to declare, that the Disclosure of his Name was, by his own Desire, reserved till the Publication of the Piece.

Both the Authors, however, who have before been separately honoured with the Indulgence of the Publick, now beg Leave to make their joint Acknowledgements for the very favourable Reception of the CLANDESTINE MARRIAGE.

PROLOGUE.

Written by Mr. GARRICK.

Spoken by Mr. HOLLAND.

POETS and Painters, who from Nature draw
    Their best and richest Stores, have made this Law:
That each should neighbourly assist his Brother,
And steal with Decency from one another.
To-night, your matchless Hogarth gives the Thought,
Which from his Canvas to the Stage is brought.
And who so fit to warm the Poet's Mind,
As he who pictur'd Morals and Mankind?
But not the same their Characters and Scenes;
Both labour for one End, by different Means;
Each, as it suits him, takes a separate Road,
Their one great Object, MARRIAGE-A-LA-MODE!
Where Titles deign with Cits to have and hold,
And change rich Blood for more substantial Gold!
And honour'd Trade from Interest turns aside,
To hazard Happiness for titled Pride.
The Painter dead, yet still he charms the Eye;
While England lives, his Fame can never die:
But he, who struts his Hour upon the Stage,
Can scarce extend his Fame for Half an Age;
Nor Pen nor Pencil can the Actor save,
The Art, and Artist, share one common Grave.
  O let me drop one tributary Tear,
On poor Jack Falstaff's Grave, and Juliet's Bier!
You to their Worth must Testimony give;
'Tis in your Hearts alone their Fame can live.
Still as the Scenes of Life will shift away,
The strong Impressions of their Art decay.
Your Children cannot feel what you have known;
They'll boast of QUINS and CIBBERS of their own:
The greatest Glory of our happy few,
Is to be felt, and be approv'd by YOU.

Dramatis Personæ.

Lord Ogleby,	*Mr.* KING.
Sir John Melvil,	*Mr.* HOLLAND.
Sterling,	*Mr.* YATES.
Lovewell,	*Mr.* POWELL.
Canton,	*Mr.* BADDELEY.
Brush,	*Mr.* PALMER.
Serjeant Flower,	*Mr.* LOVE.
Traverse,	*Mr.* LEE.
Trueman,	*Mr.* AICKIN.
Mrs. Heidelberg,	*Mrs.* CLIVE.
Miss Sterling,	*Miss* POPE.
Fanny,	*Mrs.* PALMER.
Betty,	*Mrs.* ————
Chamber-maid,	*Miss* PLYM.
Trusty,	*Miss* MILLS.

THE
Clandeſtine Marriage,

A

C O M E D Y.

ACT I.

SCENE, *A room in* Sterling's *houſe.*
Miſs Fanny *and* Betty *meeting.*

Betty *running in.*

MA'am! Miſs Fanny! Ma'am!

Fanny. What's the matter! Betty!

Betty. Oh la! Ma'am! as ſure as I am alive, here is your huſband—

Fanny. Huſh! my dear Betty! if any body in the houſe ſhould hear you, I am ruined.

Betty. Mercy on me! it has frighted me to ſuch a degree, that my heart is come up to my mouth.—But as I was a ſaying, Ma'am, here's that dear, ſweet—

Fanny. Have a care! Betty.

Betty. Lord! I'm bewitched, I think.—But as I was a ſaying, Ma'am, here's Mr. Lovewell juſt come from London.

Fanny. Indeed!

Betty. Yes, indeed, and indeed, Ma'am, he is. I ſaw him croſſing the court-yard in his boots.

Fanny. I am glad to hear it.—But pray now, my dear Betty, be cautious. Don't mention that word

B   again,

again, on any account.---You know, we have agreed never to drop any expressions of that sort for fear of an accident.

Betty. Dear Ma'am, you may depend upon me. There is not a more trustier creature on the face of the earth, than I am. Though I say it, I am as secret as the grave---and if it's never told, till I tell it, it may remain untold till dooms-day for Betty.

Fanny. I know you are faithful---but in our circumstances we cannot be too careful.

Betty. Very true, Ma'am!---and yet I vow and protest, there's more plague than pleasure with a secret; especially if a body may'nt mention it to four or five of one's particular acquaintance.

Fanny. Do but keep this secret a little while longer, and then, I hope you may mention it to any body.--- Mr. Lovewell will acquaint the family with the nature of our situation as soon as possible.

Betty. The sooner the better, I believe: for if he does not tell it, there's a little tell-tale, I know of, will come and tell it for him.

Fanny. Fie, Betty!   [*blushing.*

Betty. Ah! you may well blush.---But you're not so sick, and so pale, and so wan, and so many qualms---

Fanny. Have done! I shall be quite angry with you.

Betty. Angry!---Bless the dear puppet! I am sure I shall love it, as much as if it was my own.---I meant no harm, heaven knows.

Fanny. Well, say no more of this.---It makes me uneasy---All I have to ask of you, is to be faithful and secret, and not to reveal this matter, till we disclose it to the family ourselves.

Betty. Me reveal it!---If I say a word, I wish I may be burned. I would not do you any harm for the world---And as for Mr. Lovewell, I am sure I have loved the dear gentleman, ever since he got a tide-waiter's place for my brother---But let me tell you both, you must leave off your soft looks to each

other,

other, and your whispers, and your glances, and your always sitting next to one another at dinner, and your long walks together in the evening.---For my part, if I had not been in the secret, I shou'd have known you were a pair of loviers at least, if not man and wife, as——

Fanny. See there now! again. Pray be careful.

Betty. Well---well---nobody hears me.---Man and wife.---I'll say no more---what I tell you is very true for all that---

Lovewell. [*calling within.*] William!

Betty. Hark! I hear your husband---.

Fanny. What!

Betty. I say, here comes Mr. Lovewell---Mind the caution I give you---I'll be whipped now, if you are not the first person he sees or speaks to in the family---However, if you chuse it, it's nothing at all to me---as you sow, you must reap---as you brew, so you must bake.---I'll e'en slip down the back-stairs, and leave you together.   [*Exit.*

Fanny *alone.*

I see, I see I shall never have a moment's ease till our marriage is made public. New distresses croud in upon me every day. The solicitude of my mind sinks my spirits, preys upon my health, and destroys every comfort of my life. It shall be revealed, let what will be the consequence.

Enter Lovewell.

Lovew. My love!---How's this?---In tears?---Indeed this is too much. You promised me to support your spirits, and to wait the determination of our fortune with patience.---For my sake, for your own, be comforted! Why will you study to add to our uneasiness and perplexity?

Fanny. Oh, Mr. Lovewell! the indelicacy of a secret marriage grows every day more and more shocking to me. I walk about the house like a guilty wretch: I imagine myself the object of the suspicion of the whole family ; and am under the perpetual terrors of a fhameful detection.

Lovew. Indeed, indeed, you are to blame. The amiable delicacy of your temper, and your quick fenfibility, only ferve to make you unhappy.---To clear up this affair properly to Mr. Sterling, is the continual employment of my thoughts. Every thing now is in a fair train. It begins to grow ripe for a difcovery; and I have no doubt of its concluding to the fatisfaction of ourfelves, of your father, and the whole family.

Fanny. End how it will, I am refolved it fhall end foon---very foon.---I wou'd not live another week in this agony of mind to be miftrefs of the univerfe.

Lovew. Do not be too violent neither. Do not let us difturb the joy of your fifter's marriage with the tumult this matter may occafion!---I have brought letters from Lord Ogleby and Sir John Melvil to Mr. Sterling---They will be here this evening---and, I dare fay, within this hour.

Fanny. I am forry for it.

Lovew. Why fo ?

Fanny. No matter---Only let us difclofe our marriage immediately !

Lovew. As foon as poffible.

Fanny. But directly.

Lovew. In a few days, you may depend on it.

Fanny. To-night---or to-morrow morning.

Lovew. That, I fear, will be impracticable.

Fanny. Nay, but you muft.

Lovew. Muft! why ?

Fanny. Indeed, you muft.---I have the moft alarming reafons for it.

Lovew. Alarming indeed! for they alarm me, even before I am acquainted with them---What are they ?

Fanny. I cannot tell you.

Lovew. Not tell me ?

Fanny. Not at prefent. When all is fettled, you fhall be acquainted with every thing.

Lovew.

Lovew. Sorry they are coming!---Muſt be diſcovered!---What can this mean!---Is it poſſible you can have any reaſons that need be concealed from me?

Fanny. Do not diſturb yourſelf with conjectures--- but reſt aſſured, that though you are unable to divine the cauſe, the conſequence of a diſcovery, be it what it will, cannot be attended with half the miſeries of the preſent interval.

Lovew. You put me upon the rack.---I wou'd do any thing to make you eaſy.---But you know your father's temper.---Money (you will excuſe my frankneſs) is the ſpring of all his actions, which nothing but the idea of acquiring nobility or magnificence can ever make him forego---and theſe he thinks his money will purchaſe.---You know too your aunt's, Mrs. Heidelberg's, notions of the ſplendor of high life, her contempt for every thing that does not reliſh of what ſhe calls Quality, and that from the vaſt fortune in her hands, by her late huſband, ſhe abſolutely governs Mr. Sterling and the whole family: now, if they ſhould come to the knowledge of this affair too abruptly, they might, perhaps, be incenſed beyond all hopes of reconciliation.

Fanny. But if they are made acquainted with it otherwiſe than by ourſelves, it will be ten times worſe: and a diſcovery grows every day more probable. The whole family have long ſuſpected our affection. We are alſo in the power of a fooliſh maid-ſervant; and if we may even depend on her fidelity, we cannot anſwer for her diſcretion.---Diſcover it therefore immediately, leſt ſome accident ſhould bring it to light, and involve us in additional diſgrace.

Lovew. Well---well---I meant to diſcover it ſoon, but would not do it too precipitately.---I have more than once ſounded Mr. Sterling about it, and will attempt him more ſeriouſly the next opportunity. But my principal hopes are theſe.---My relationſhip to Lord Ogleby, and his having placed me with your father, have, been, you know, the firſt links in the chain of this connection between the two families; in conſequence of which, I am at preſent in high favour with all parties: while they all remain thus well-affected to me, I propoſe to lay our caſe before the old Lord; and if I can prevail on him to me-diate in this affair, I make no doubt but he will be able to appeaſe your father; and, being a lord and a man of quality, I am ſure he may bring Mrs. Heidelberg into good-humour at any time.---Let me beg you, therefore, to have but a little patience, as, you ſee, we are upon the very eve of a diſcovery, that muſt probably be to our advantage.

Fanny. Manage it your own way. I am per-ſuaded.

Lovew. But in the mean time make yourſelf eaſy.

Fanny. As eaſy as I can, I will.—We had better not remain together any longer at preſent.—Think of this buſineſs, and let me know how you proceed.

Lovew. Depend on my care! But, pray, be chearful.

Fanny. I will.

As ſhe is going out, enter Sterling.

Ster. Hey-day! who have we got here?

Fanny. [*confuſed.*] Mr. Lovewell, Sir!

Sterl. And where are you going, huſſey?

Fanny. To my ſiſter's chamber, Sir! [*Exit.*

Sterl. Ah, Lovewell! What! always getting my fooliſh girl yonder into a corner?—Well—well—let us but once ſee her elder ſiſter faſt-married to Sir John Melvil, we'll ſoon provide a good huſband for Fanny, I warrant you.

Lovew. Wou'd to heaven, Sir, you would provide her one of my recommendation!

Sterl. Yourſelf? eh, Lovewell!

Lovew. With your pleaſure, Sir!

Sterl. Mighty well!

Lovew.

Lovew. And I flatter myfelf, that fuch a propofal would not be very difagreeable to Mifs Fanny.

Sterl. Better and better!

Lovew. And if I could but obtain your confent, Sir——

Sterl. What! you marry Fanny!---no---no---that will never do, Lovewell!—You're a good boy, to be fure—I have a great value for you—but can't think of you for a fon-in-law,—There's no *Stuff,* in the cafe, no money, Lovewell!

Lovew. My pretenfions to fortune, indeed, are but moderate: but though not equal to fplendor, fufficient to keep us above diftrefs.—Add to which, that I hope by diligence to increafe it---and have love, honour——

Sterl. But not the *Stuff*, Lovewell!—Add one little round o. to the fum total of your fortune, and that will be the fineft thing you can fay to me.—You know I've a regard for you—would do any thing to ferve you—any thing on the footing of friendfhip— but—

Lovew. If you think me worthy of your friend-fhip, Sir, be affured, that there is no inftance in which I fhould rate your friendfhip fo highly.

Sterl. Pfha! pfha! that's another thing, you know.—Where money or intereft is concerned, friend-fhip is quite out of the queftion.

Lovew. But where the happinefs of a daughter is at ftake, you wou'd not fcruple, fure, to facrifice a little to her inclinations.

Sterl. Inclinations! why, you wou'd not perfuade me that the girl is in love with you---eh, Lovewell!

Lovew. I cannot abfolutely anfwer for Mifs Fanny, Sir; but am fure that the chief happinefs or mifery of my life depends entirely upon her.

Sterl. Why, indeed now if your kinfman, Lord Ogleby, would come down handfomely for you--- but that's impoffible---No, no---'twill never do---I

muft

muſt hear no more of this---Come, Lovewell, promiſe me that I ſhall hear no more of this.

Lovew. [*heſitating.*] I am afraid, Sir, I ſhou'd not
be able to keep my word with you, if I did promiſe
you.

Sterl. Why you wou'd not offer to marry her without my conſent! wou'd you, Lovewell?

Lovew. Marry her, Sir!   [*confuſed.*

Sterl. Ay, marry her, Sir!---I know very well that
a warm ſpeech or two from ſuch a dangerous young
ſpark, as you are, would go much farther towards per-
ſuading a ſilly girl to do what ſhe has more than a
month's mind to do, than twenty grave lectures
from fathers or mothers, or uncles or aunts, to prevent her.---But you wou'd not, ſure, be ſuch a baſe
fellow, ſuch a treacherous young rogue, as to ſeduce
my daughter's affections, and deſtroy the peace of
my family in that manner.---I muſt inſiſt on it, that
you give me your word not to marry her without my
conſent.

Lovew. Sir---I---I---as to that---I---I---I beg, Sir---
Pray, Sir, excuſe me on this ſubject at preſent.

Sterl. Promiſe then, that you will carry this matter
no further without my approbation.

Lovew. You may depend on it, Sir, that it ſhall
go no further.

Sterl. Well---well---that's enough---I'll take care
of the reſt, I warrant you.---Come, come, let's have
done with this nonſenſe!---What's doing in town?---
Any news upon 'Change?

Lovew. Nothing material.

Sterl. Have you ſeen the currants, the ſoap, and
Madeira, ſafe in the warehouſes? Have you com-
pared the goods with the invoice and bills of lading,
and are they all right?

Lovew. They are, Sir!

Sterl. And how are ſtocks?

Lovew. Fell one and a half this morning.

Sterl.

Sterl. Well---well---some good news from America, and they'll be up again.---But how are Lord Ogelby and Sir John Melvil? When are we to expect them?

Lovew. Very soon, Sir. I came on purpose to bring you their commands. Here are letters from both of them. [*giving letters.*

Sterl. Let me see---let me see---'Slife, how his Lordship's letter is perfumed!---It takes my breath away.---[*opening it.*] And French paper too! with a fine border of flowers and flourishes---and a slippery glofs on it that dazzles one's eyes.---*My dear Mr. Sterling.*---[*reading.*]---Mercy on me! His Lordship writes a worfe hand than a boy at his exercife.--- But how's this?---Eh!---*with you to night*---[*reading.*] --- *Lawyers to-morrow morning* --- To-night! --- that's fudden indeed. --- Where's my fifter Heidelberg? fhe fhou'd know of this immediately.---Here, John! Harry! Thomas! [*calling the fervants.*] Hark ye, Lovewell!

Lovew. Sir!

Sterl. Mind now, how I'll entertain his Lordship and Sir John---We'll fhew your fellows at the other end of the town how we live in the city---They fhall eat gold---and drink gold---and lie in gold---Here cook! butler! [*calling.*] What fignifies your birth and education, and titles? Money, money, that's the ftuff that makes the great man in this country.

Lovew. Very true, Sir!

Sterl. True, Sir? --- Why then have done with your nonfenfe of love and matrimony. You're not rich enough to think of a wife yet. A man of bufinefs fhou'd mind nothing but his bufinefs.--- Where are thefe fellows? John! Thomas! [*calling.*] ---Get an eftate, and a wife will follow of courfe. ------Ah! Lovewell! An Englifh merchant is the moft refpectable character in the univerfe. 'Slife, man, a rich Englifh merchant may make himfelf a

match

match for the daughter of a nabob.—Where are all my rascals? Here, William!   [*Exit calling.*

Lovewell *alone.*

So!—As I suspected.—Quite averse to the match, and likely to receive the news of it with great displeasure.—What's best to be done?—Let me see!—Suppose I get Sir John Melvil to interest himself in this affair. He may mention it to Lord Ogelby with a better grace than I can, and more probably prevail on him to interfere in it. I can open my mind also more freely to Sir John. He told me, when I left him in town, that he had something of consequence to communicate, and that I could be of use to him. I am glad of it: for the confidence he reposes in me, and the service I may do him, will ensure me his good offices.—Poor Fanny! It hurts me to see her so uneasy, and her making a mystery of the cause adds to my anxiety.—Something must be done upon her account; for at all events, her sollicitude shall be removed.   [*Exit.*

Scene changes to another chamber.

Enter Miss Sterling, *and* Miss Fanny.

Miss Sterl. Oh, my dear sister, say no more! This is downright hypocrisy.—You shall never convince me that you don't envy me beyond measure.—Well, after all, it is extremely natural—It is impossible to be angry with you.

Fanny. Indeed, sister, you have no cause.

Miss Sterl. And you really pretend not to envy me?

Fanny. Not in the least.

Miss Sterl. And you don't in the least wish that you was just in my situation?

Fanny. No, indeed, I don't. Why should I?

Miss Sterl. Why should you? What! on the brink of marriage, fortune, title—But I had forgot.
—There's

—There's that dear sweet creature Mr. Lovewell in the case.—You would not break your faith with your true love now for the world, I warrant you.

Fanny. Mr. Lovewell!—always Mr. Lovewell!—Lord, what signifies Mr. Lovewell, sister?

Miss Sterl. Pretty peevish soul!—Oh, my dear, grave, romantic sister!—a perfect philosopher in petticoats!—Love and a cottage!—Eh, Fanny!—Ah, give me indifference and a coach and six!—

Fanny. And why not the coach and six without the indifference?—But, pray, when is this happy marriage of your's to be celebrated?—I long to give you joy.

Miss Sterl. In a day or two—I can't tell exactly.—Oh, my dear sister!—I must mortify her a little. [*aside.*]—I know you have a pretty taste. Pray, give me your opinion of my jewels.—How d'ye like the stile of this esclavage? [*shewing jewels.*

Fanny. Extremely handsome indeed, and well fancied.

Miss Sterl. What d'ye think of these bracelets? I shall have a miniature of my father, set round with diamonds, to one, and Sir John's to the other.—And this pair of ear-rings! set transparent!—here, the tops, you see, will take off to wear in a morning, or in an undress—how d'ye like them?

[*shews jewels.*

Fanny. Very much, I assure you—Bless me, sister, you have a prodigious quantity of jewels—you'll be the very Queen of Diamonds.

Miss Sterl. Ha! ha! ha! very well, my dear!—I shall be as fine as a little queen indeed.—I have a bouquet to come home to-morrow — made up of diamonds, and rubies, and emeralds, and topazes, and amethysts — jewels of all colours, green, red, blue, yellow, intermixt—the prettiest thing you ever saw in your life!—The jeweller says, I shall set out with as many diamonds as any body in town, except

Lady

Lady Brilliant, and Polly *What d'ye call-it*, Lord Squander's kept miſtreſs.

Fanny. But what are your wedding-cloaths, ſiſter?

Miſs Sterl. Oh, white and ſilver, to be ſure, you know.—I bought them at Sir Joſeph Luteſtring's, and ſat above an hour in the parlour behind the ſhop, conſulting Lady Luteſtring about gold and ſilver ſtuffs, on purpoſe to mortify her.

Fanny. Fie, ſiſter! how could you be ſo abominably provoking?

Miſs Sterl. Oh, I have no patience with the pride of your city-knights' ladies.—Did you never obſerve the airs of Lady Luteſtring dreſt in the richeſt brocade out of her huſband's ſhop, playing crown-whiſt at Haberdaſher's-Hall?—While the civil ſmirking Sir Joſeph, with a ſmug wig trimmed round his broad face as cloſe as a new-cut yew-hedge, and his ſhoes ſo black that they ſhine again, ſtands all day in his ſhop, faſtened to his counter like a bad ſhilling?

Fanny. Indeed, indeed, ſiſter, this is too much—If you talk at this rate, you will be abſolutely a bye-word in the city—You muſt never venture on the inſide of Temple-Bar again.

Miſs Sterl. Never do I deſire it—never, my dear Fanny, I promiſe you.—Oh, how I long to be tranſ-ported to the dear regions of Groſvenor-Square—far —far from the dull diſtricts of Alderſgate, Cheap, Candlewick, and Farringdon Without and Within! —My heart goes pit-a-pit at the very idea of being introduced at court! —gilt chariot! — pyeballed horſes!—laced liveries!—and then the whiſpers buz-zing round the circle—" Who is that young lady? Who is ſhe?" — " Lady Melvil, Ma'am!"—Lady Melvil! my ears tingle at the ſound.—And then at dinner, inſtead of my father perpetually aſking— " Any news upon 'Change?"—to cry—Well, Sir John! any thing new from Arthur's?—or—to ſay to ſome other woman of quality, Was your Ladyſhip at

the

the Duchefs of Rubber's laft night ?—Did you call in at Lady Thunder's ? In the immenfity of croud I fwear I did not fee you—fcarce a foul at the opera laft Saturday—fhall I fee you at Carlifle-Houfe next Thurfday ?—Oh, the dear Beau-Monde ! I was born to move in the fphere of the great world.

Fanny. And fo, in the midft of all this happinefs, you have no compaffion for me—no pity for us poor mortals in common life.

Mifs Sterl. [*affectedly.*] You ?—You're above pity. —You would not change conditions with me—You're over head and ears in love, you know.—Nay, for that matter, if Mr. Lovewell and you come together, as I doubt not you will, you will live very comfortably, I dare fay.—He will mind his bufinefs— you'll employ yourfelf in the delightful care of your family—and once in a feafon perhaps you'll fit together in a front-box at a benefit play, as we ufed to do at our dancing-mafter's, you know—and perhaps I may meet you in the fummer with fome other citizens at Tunbridge.—For my part, I fhall always entertain a proper regard for my relations.—You fha'n't want my countenance, I affure you.

Fanny. Oh, you're too kind, fifter !

Enter Mrs. Heidelberg.

Mrs. Heidel. [*at entering.*] Here this evening !— I vow and perteft we fhall fcarce have time to provide for them—Oh, my dear ! [*to Mifs Sterl.*] I am glad to fee you're not quite in a difh-abille. Lord Ogleby and Sir John Melvil will be here to-night.

Mifs Sterl. To-night, Ma'am ?

Mrs. Heidel. Yes, my dear, to-night.—Do, put on a fmarter cap, and change thofe ordinary ruffles ! —Lord, I have fuch a deal to do, I fhall fcarce have time to flip on my Italian luteftring.—Where is this dawdle of a houfekeeper?—[*Enter Mrs. Trufty.*] Oh, here, Trufty ! do you know that people of quality are expected here this evening ?

Trufty.

Trusty. Yes, Ma'am.

Mrs. Heidel. Well—Do you be sure now that every thing is done in the most genteelest manner—and to the honour of the famaly.

Trusty. Yes, Ma'am.

Mrs. Heidel. Well—but mind what I say to you.

Trusty. Yes, Ma'am.

Mrs. Heidel. His Lordship is to lie in the chintz bedchamber—d'ye hear?—And Sir John in the blue damask room—His Lordship's valet-de-shamb in the opposite——

Trusty. But Mr. Lovewell is come down—and you know that's his room, Ma'am.

Mrs. Heidel. Well—well—Mr. Lovewell may make shift—or get a bed at the George.—But hark ye, Trusty!

Trusty. Ma'am!

Mrs. Heidel. Get the great dining-room in order as soon as possable. Unpaper the curtains, take the civers off the couch and the chairs, and put the china figures on the mantle-piece immediately.

Trusty. Yes, Ma'am.

Mrs. Heidel. Be gone then! fly, this instant!—Where's my brother Sterling—

Trusty. Talking to the butler, Ma'am.

Mrs. Heidel. Very well. [*Exit* Trusty.] Miss Fanny!—I pertest I did not see you before—Lord, child, what's the matter with you?

Fanny. With me? Nothing, Ma'am.

Mrs. Heidel. Bless me! Why your face is as pale, and black, and yellow—of fifty colours, I pertest.—And then you have dreft yourself as loose and as big—I declare there is not such a thing to be seen now, as a young woman with a fine waist—You all make yourselves as round as Mrs. Deputy Barter. Go, child!—You know the qualaty will be here by and by—Go, and make yourself a little more fit to be seen. [*Exit* Fanny.] She is gone away in tears—absolutely crying, I vow and pertest.—This ridicalous Love! we

must

muft put a ftop to it. It makes a perfect nataral of the girl.

Mifs Sterl. Poor foul! fhe can't help it. [*affectedly.*

Mrs. Heidel. Well, my dear! Now I fhall have an opportoonity of convincing you of the abfurdity of what you was telling me concerning Sir John Melvil's behaviour to you.

Mifs Sterl. Oh, it gives me no manner of uneafinefs. But, indeed, Ma'am, I cannot be perfuaded but that Sir John is an extremely cold lover. Such diftant civility, grave looks, and lukewarm profeffions of efteem for me and the whole family! I have heard of flames and darts, but Sir John's is a paffion of mere ice and fnow.

Mrs. Heidel. Oh, fie, my dear! I am perfetly afhamed of you. That's fo like the notions of your poor fifter! What you complain of as coldnefs and indiffarence, is nothing but the extreme gentilaty of his addrefs, an exact pictur of the manners of qualaty.

Mifs Sterl. Oh, he is the very mirror of complaifance! full of formal bows and fet fpeeches!—I declare, if there was any violent paffion on my fide, I fhould be quite jealous of him.

Mrs. Heidel. I fay jealus indeed—Jealus of who, pray?

Mifs Sterl. My fifter Fanny. She feems a much greater favourite than I am, and he pays her infinitely more attention, I affure you.

Mrs. Heidel. Lord! d'ye think a man of fafhion, as he is, can't diftinguifh between the genteel and the wulgar part of the famaly?—Between you and your fifter, for inftance—or me and my brother?—Be advifed by me, child! It is all pulitenefs and good-breeding.—Nobody knows the qualaty better than I do.

Mifs Sterl. In my mind the old lord, his uncle, has ten times more gallantry about him than Sir John. He is full of attentions to the ladies, and
fmiles,

smiles, and grins, and leers, and ogles, and fills every wrinkle in his old wizen face with comical expressions of tenderness. I think he would make an admirable Sweetheart.

Enter Sterling.

Sterl. [*at entering.*] No fish?—Why the pond was dragged but yesterday morning—There's carp and tench in the boat.—Pox on't, if that dog Lovewell had any thought, he wou'd have brought down a turbot, or some of the land-carriage mackarel.

Mrs. Heidel. Lord, brother, I am afraid his Lordship and Sir John will not arrive while it is light.

Sterl. I warrant you.—But, pray, sister Heidelberg, let the turtle be drest to-morrow, and some venison—and let the gardener cut some pine-apples—and get out some ice.—I'll answer for wine, I warrant you—I'll give them such a glass of Champagne as they never drank in their lives—no, not at a duke's table.

Mrs. Heidel. Pray now, brother, mind how you behave. I am always in a fright about you with people of qualaty. Take care that you don't fall asleep directly after supper, as you commonly do. Take a good deal of snuff; and that will keep you awake—And don't burst out with your horrible loud horse-laughs. It is monstrous wulgar.

Sterl. Never fear, sister!—Who have we here?

Mrs. Heidel. It is Monf. Cantoon, the Swish gentleman, that lives with his Lordship, I vow and pertest.

Enter Canton.

Sterl. Ah, Mounseer! your servant.—I am very glad to see you, Mounseer.

Canton. Mosh oblige to Monf. Sterling.—Ma'am, I am yours—Matemoifelle, I am yours. [*bowing round.*

Mrs. Heidel. Your humble servant, Mr. Cantoon!

Canton. I kiss your hands, Matam!

Sterl. Well, Mounseer!—and what news of your good family!—when are we to see his Lordship and Sir John?

Canton.

Canton. Monf. Sterling! Milor Ogelby and Sir Jean Melvile will be here in one quarter-hour.

Sterl. I am glad to hear it.

Mrs. Heidel. O; I am perdigious glad to hear it. Being fo late I was afeard of fome accident.—Will you pleafe to have any thing, Mr. Cantoon, after your journey?

Canton. No, I tank you, Ma'am.

Mrs. Heidel. Shall I go and fhew you the apart-ments, Sir?

Canton. You do me great honeur, Ma'am.

Mrs. Heidel. Come then!—come, my dear! [*to Mifs* Sterling.] [*Exeunt.*

Manet Sterling.

Sterl. Pox on't, it's almoft dark—It will be too late to go round the garden this evening.—However, I will carry them to take a peep at my fine canal at leaft, I am determined. [*Exit.*

ACT II. SCENE I.

SCENE, *an anti-chamber to Lord* Ogleby's *bed-chamber—Table with chocolate, and fmall cafe for medicines.*

Enter Brufh, *my Lord's valet-de-chambre, and* Sterling's *chamber-maid.*

Brufh. YOU fhall ftay, my dear, I infift upon it.

Ch. Maid. Nay, pray, Sir, don't be fo pofitive; I can't ftay indeed.

Brufh. You fhall take one cup to our better ac-quaintance.

Ch. Maid. I feldom drinks chocolate; and if I did, one has no fatisfaction, with fuch apprehenfions about one—if my Lord fhould wake, or the Swifh gentle-man fhould fee one, or Madam Heidelberg fhould

C know

know of it, I fhould be frighted to death—befides, I have had my tea already this morning—I'm fure I hear my Lord. *[in a fright.*

Brufh. No, no, Madam, don't flutter yourfelf— the moment my Lord wakes, he rings his bell, which I anfwer fooner or later, as it fuits my convenience.

Ch. Maid. But fhould he come upon us without ringing—

Brufh. I'll forgive him if he does—This key [*takes a phial out of the cafe.*] locks him up till I pleafe to let him out.

Ch. Maid. Law, Sir! that's potecary's ftuff.

Brufh. It is fo—but without this he can no more get out of bed—than he can read without fpectacles— [*fips.*] What with qualms, age, rheumatifm, and a few furfeits in his youth, he muft have a great deal of brufhing, oyling, fcrewing, and winding up to fet him a going for the day.

Ch. Maid. [*fips.*] That's prodigious indeed—[*fips.*] My Lord feems quite in a decay.

Brufh. Yes, he's quite a fpectacle, [*fips.*] a mere corpfe, till he is reviv'd and refrefh'd from our little magazine here—When the reftorative pills, and cordial waters warm his ftomach, and get into his head, vanity frifks in his heart, and then he fets up for the lover, the rake, and the fine gentleman.

Ch. Maid. [*fips.*] Poor gentleman!—but fhould the Swifh gentleman come upon us. [*frighten'd.*

Brufh. Why then the Englifh gentleman would be very angry—No foreigner muft break in upon my privacy. [*fips.*] But I can affure you Monfieur Canton is otherwife employ'd.—He is oblig'd to fkim the cream of half a fcore news-papers for my Lord's breakfaft—ha! ha! ha! Pray, Madam, drink your cup peaceably—My Lord's chocolate is remarkably good, he won't touch a drop but what comes from Italy.

Ch.

Ch. Maid. [*sipping.*] 'Tis very fine indeed !—[*sips.*] and charmingly perfum'd—it smells for all the world like our young ladies dressing-boxes.

Brush. You have an excellent taste, Madam, and I must beg of you to accept of a few cakes for your own drinking, [*takes 'em out of a drawer in the table.*] and in return, I desire nothing but to taste the perfume of your lips—[*kisses her.*]—A small return of favours, Madam, will make, I hope, this country, and retirement agreeable to both. [*he bows, she curtsies.*] Your young ladies are fine girls, faith : [*sips.*] tho', upon my soul, I am quite of my old lord's mind about them, and were I inclin'd to matrimony, I should take the youngest. [*sips.*

Ch. Maid. Miss Fanny's the most affablest and the most best nater'd creter !

Brush. And the eldest a little haughty or so——

Ch. Maid. More haughtier and prouder than Saturn himself—but this I say quite confidential to you, for one would not hurt a young lady's marriage, you know. [*sips.*

Brush. By no means, but you can't hurt it with us—we don't consider tempers—we want money, Mrs. Nancy—give us enough of that, we'll abate you a great deal in other particulars—ha! ha! ha!

Ch. Maid. Bless me, here's somebody—[*bell rings.*] —O ! 'tis my Lord—Well, your servant, Mr. Brush— I'll clean the cups in the next room.

Brush. Do so—but never mind the bell—I shan't go this half hour. Will you drink tea with me in the afternoon ?

Ch. Maid. Not for the world, Mr. Brush—I'll be here to set all things to rights—but I must not drink tea indeed—and so your servant. [*Exit Maid with tea-*
[*Bell rings again.*] board.

Brush. It is impossible to stupify one's self in the country for a week without some little flirting with the Abigails : this is much the handsomest wench in the house, except the old citizen's youngest

C 2 daughter,

daughter, and I have not time enough to lay a plan for Her—[*bell rings.*] And now I'll go to my Lord, for I have nothing else to do. [*Exit.*

Enter Canton with news-papers in his hand.

Cant. Monsieur Bruth—Maitre Bruth—My Lor stirra yet?

Bruth. He has just rung his bell—I am going to him.

Cant. Depechez vous donc. [*Exit Bruth.*
[*puts on spectacles.*] I wish the Deviel had all dese papiers—I forget as fast as I read. De Advertise put out of my head de Gazette, de Gazette de Chronique, and so dey all go l'un aprés l'autre—I must get some nouvelle for my Lor, or he'll be enragé contre moi—Voyons!—[*reads in the papers.*] Here is nothing but Anti Sejanus & advertise—

Enter Maid with chocolate things.

Vat you vant, child?—

Ch. Maid. Only the chocolate things, Sir.

Cant. O ver well—dat is good girl—and ver pritt too! [*Exit Maid.*

Lord Ogleby within.

Lord Ogle. Canton, he, he—[*laughs.*]—Canton!

Cant. I come, my Lor—vat shall I do?—I have no news—He will make great tintamarre!—

Lord Ogle. [*within.*] Canton, I say, Canton! Where are you?

Enter Lord Ogleby leaning on Bruth.

Cant. Here, my Lor, I ask pardon, my Lor, I have not finish de papiers—

Lord Ogle. Dem your pardon, and your papiers—I want you here, Canton.

Cant. Den I run, dat is all—[*Pushes along—Lord Ogleby leans upon Canton too, and comes forward.*

Lord Ogle. You Swiss are the most unaccountable mixture—you have the language and the impertinence of the French, with the laziness of Dutchmen.

Cant.

Cant. 'Tis very true, my Lor—I can't help—

Lord Ogle. [*cries out.*] O Diavolo!

Cant. You are not in pain, I hope, my Lor.

Lord Ogle. Indeed but I am, my Lor—That vulgar fellow Sterling, with his city politenefs, would force me down his flope laft night to fee a clay-colour'd ditch, which he calls a canal; and what with the dew, and the eaft-wind, my hips and fhoulders are abfolutely fcrew'd to my body.

Cant. A littel veritable eau d'arquibufade vil fet all to right again—

        [*my Lord fits down,* Brufh *gives chocolate.*

Lord Ogle. Where are the palfy-drops, Brufh?

Brufh. Here, my Lord!   [*pouring out.*

Lord Ogle. Quelle nouvelle avez vous, Canton?

Cant. A great deal of papier, but no news at all.

Lord Ogle. What! nothing at all, you ftupid fellow?

Cant. Yes, my Lor, I have little advertife here vil give you more plaifir den all de lyes about nothing at all. La voila!   [*puts on his fpectacles.*

Lord Ogle. Come read it, Canton, with good emphafis, and good difcretion.

Cant. I vil, my Lor.—[*Cant. reads.*] Dere is no queftion, but that the Cofmetique Royale vil utterlie take away all heats, pimps, frecks & oder eruptions of de fkin, and likewife de wrinque of old age, &c. &c.---A great deal more, my Lor---be fure to afk for de Cofmetique Royale, figned by de Docteur own hand---Dere is more raifon for dis caution dan good men vil tink---Eh bien, my Lor!

Lord Ogle. Eh bien, Canton!--Will you purchafe any?

Cant. For you, my Lor?

Lord Ogle. For me, you old puppy! for what?

Cant. My Lor?

Lord Ogle. Do I want cofmeticks?

Cant. My Lor?

Lord Ogle. Look in my face---come, be fincere.--- Does it want the affiftance of art?

       Cant.

Cant. [*with his fpectacles.*] En verité non.---'Tis very fmoofe and brillian---but I tote dat you might take a like by way of prevention.

Lord Ogle. You thought like an old fool, Monfieur, as you generally do——The furfeit-water, Brufh ! [Brufh *pours out.*] What do you think, Brufh, of this family, we are going to be connected with ?---Eh !

Brufh. Very well to marry in, my Lord ; but it would not do to live with.

Lord Ogle. You are right, Brufh---There is no wafh-ing the Blackamoor white---Mr. Sterling will never get rid of Black-Fryars, always tafte of the Borachio ---and the poor woman his fifter is fo bufy and fo notable, to make one welcome, that I have not yet got over her firft reception ; it almoft amounted to fuffocation ! I think the daughters are tolerable--- Where's my cephalick fnuff? [Brufh *gives him a box.*

Cant. Dey tink fo of you, my Lor, for dey look at noting elfe, ma foi.

Lord Ogle. Did they ?---Why, I think they did a lit-tle---Where's my glafs ? [Brufh *puts one on the table.*] The youngeft is delectable. [*takes fnuff.*

Cant. O, ouy, my Lor---very delect, inteed ; fhe made doux yeux at you, my Lor.

Lord Ogle. She was particular---the eldeft, my ne-phew's lady, will be a moft valuable wife ; fhe has all the vulgar fpirits of her father, and aunt, happily blended with the termagant qualities of her deceafed mother.---Some pepper-mint water, Brufh !---How happy is it, Cant. for young ladies in general, that people of quality overlook every thing in a marriage contract, but their fortune !

Cant. C'eft bien heureux, et commode auffi.

Lord Ogle. Brufh, give me that pamphlet by my bed-fide---[Brufh *goes for it.*] Canton, do you wait in the anti-chamber, and let nobody interrupt me till I call you,

Cant. Mufh goot may do your Lordfhip !

Lord

Lord Ogle. [*to* Brufh, *who brings the pamphlet.*] And now, Brufh, leave me a little to my ftudies. [*Exit* Brufh.

Lord Ogleby *alone.*

What can I poffibly do among thefe women here, with this confounded rheumatifm? It is a moft grievous enemy to gallantry and addrefs---[*gets off his chair.*]---He!---Courage, my Lor! by heav'ns, I'm another creature---[*hums and dances a little.*] It will do, faith---Bravo, my Lor! thefe girls have abfolutely infpir'd me---If they are for a game of romps---Me voila pret! [*fings and dances.*] O---that's an ugly twinge---but it's gone.---I have rather too much of the lily this morning in my complexion; a faint tincture of the rofe will give a delicate fpirit to my eyes for the day. [*unlocks a drawer at the bottom of the glafs, and takes out rouge; while he's painting himfelf, a knocking at the door.*] Who's there? I won't be difturb'd.

Canton. [*without.*] My Lor, my Lor, here is Monfieur Sterling to pay his devoir to you this morn in your chambre.

Lord Ogle. [*foftly.*] What a fellow!---[*aloud.*] I am extremely honour'd by Mr. Sterling---Why don't you fee him in, Monfieur!---I wifh he was at the bottom of his ftinking canal---[*door opens.*] Oh, my dear Mr. Sterling, you do me a great deal of honour.

Enter Sterling, *and* Lovewell.

Sterl. I hope, my Lord, that your Lordfhip flept well in the night---I believe there are no better beds in Europe than I have---I fpare no pains to get 'em, nor money to buy 'em---His Majefty, God blefs him, don't fleep upon a better out of his palace; and if I had faid *in* too, I hope no treafon, my Lord.

Lord Ogle. Your beds are like every thing elfe about you, incomparable!---They not only make one reft well, but give one fpirits, Mr. Sterling.

Sterl. What fay you then, my Lord, to another walk in the garden? You muft fee my water by daylight, and my walks, and my flopes, and my clumps,

C 4 and

and my bridge, and my flow'ring trees, and my bed of Dutch tulips---Matters look'd but dim laſt night, my Lord; I feel the dew in my great toe---but I would put on a cut ſhoe, that I might be able to walk you about---I may be laid up to-morrow.

Lord Ogle. I pray heaven you may! [*aſide.*

Sterl. What ſay you, my Lord!

Lord Ogle. I was ſaying, Sir, that I was in hopes of ſeeing the young ladies at breakfaſt: Mr. Sterling, they are, in my mind, the fineſt tuleps in this part of the world---he! he!

Cant. Braviſſimo, my Lor!---ha! ha! he!

Sterl. They ſhall meet your Lordſhip in the garden ---we won't loſe our walk for them; I'll take you a little round before breakfaſt, and a larger before dinner, and in the evening you ſhall go the Grand Tower, as I call it, ha! ha! ha!

Lord Ogle. Not a foot, I hope, Mr. Sterling---conſider your gout, my good friend---You'll certainly be laid by the heels for your politeneſs---he! he! he!

Cant. Ha! ha! ha!---'tis admirable!---en verité!

[*laughing very heartily.*

Sterl. If my young man [*to* Lovewell.] here, would but laugh at my jokes, which he ought to do, as Mounſeer does at yours, my Lord, we ſhould be all life and mirth.

Lord Ogle. What ſay you, Cant. will you take my kinſman into your tuition? you have certainly the moſt companionable laugh I ever met with, and never out of tune.

Cant. But when your Lordſhip is out of ſpirits.

Lord Ogle. Well ſaid, Cant.!---but here comes my nephew, to play his part.

Enter Sir John Melvil.

Well, Sir John, what news from the iſland of Love? have you been ſighing and ſerenading this morning?

Sir John. I am glad to ſee your Lordſhip in ſuch ſpirits this morning.

Lord

Lord Ogle. I'm forry to fee you fo dull, Sir---What poor things, Mr. Sterling, thefe *very* young fellows are! they make love with faces, as if they were burying the dead---though, indeed, a marriage fometimes may be properly called a burying of the living ---eh, Mr. Sterling?

Sterl. Not if they have enough to live upon, my Lord---Ha! ha! ha!

Cant. Dat is all Monfieur Sterling tink of.

Sir John. Prithee, Lovewell, come with me into the garden; I have fomething of confequence for you, and I muft communicate it directly. } *apart.*

Love. We'll go together---

If your Lordfhip and Mr. Sterling pleafe, we'll prepare the ladies to attend you in the garden.

[*Exeunt Sir* John, *and* Lovewell.

Sterl. My girls are always ready, I make 'em rife foon and to-bed early; their hufbands fhall have 'em with good conftitutions, and good fortunes, if they have nothing elfe, my Lord.

Lord Ogle. Fine things, Mr. Sterling!

Sterl. Fine things, indeed, my Lord!---Ah, my Lord, had not you run off your fpeed in your youth, you had not been fo crippled in your age, my Lord.

Lord Ogle. Very pleafant, I proteft, he, he, he.---
[*half laughing.*

Sterl. Here's Mounfeer now, I fuppofe, is pretty near your Lordfhip's ftanding; but having little to eat, and little to fpend, in his own country, he'll wear three of your Lordfhip out---eating and drinking kills us all.

Lord Ogle. Very pleafant, I proteft---What a vulgar dog! [*afide.*

Cant. My Lor fo old as me!---He is fhicken to me---and look like a boy to pauvre me.

Sterl. Ha! ha! ha! Well faid, Mounfeer---keep to that, and you'll live in any country of the world---Ha! ha! ha!---But, my Lord, I will wait upon you into the garden: we have but a little time to breakfaft

faft---I'll go for my hat and cane, fetch a little walk with you, my Lord, and then for the hot rolls and butter!   [*Exit* Sterling.

Lord Ogle. I fhall attend you with pleafure---Hot rolls and butter, in July!---I fweat with the thoughts of it---What a ftrange beaft it is!

Cant. C'eft un barbare.

Lord Ogle. He is a vulgar dog, and if there was not fo much money in the family, which I can't do with-out, I would leave him and his hot rolls and butter directly---Come along, Monfieur!

[*Exeunt Lord* Ogelby *and* Canton.

Scene changes to the garden.

Enter Sir John Melvil, *and* Lovewell.

Lovew. In my room this morning? Impoffible.

Sir John. Before five this morning, I promife you.

Lovew. On what occafion?

Sir John. I was fo anxious to difclofe my mind to you, that I could not fleep in my bed---but I found that you could not fleep neither---The bird was flown, and the neft long fince cold. --- Where was you, Lovewell?

Lovew. Pooh! prithee! ridiculous!

Sir John. Come now! which was it? Mifs Ster-ling's maid? a pretty little rogue!---or Mifs Fanny's Abigail? a fweet foul too!---or---

Lovew. Nay, nay, leave trifling, and tell me your bufinefs.

Sir John. Well, but where was you, Lovewell?

Lovew. Walking---writing---what fignifies where I was?

Sir John. Walking! yes, I dare fay. It rained as hard as it could pour. Sweet refrefhing fhowers to walk in! No, no, Lovewell.---Now would I give twenty pounds to know which of the maids———

Lovew. But your bufinefs! your bufinefs, Sir John!

.Sir

Sir John. Let me a little into the fecrets of the family.

Lovew. Pfha!

Sir John. Poor Lovewell, he can't bear it, I fee. She charged you not to kifs and tell.---Eh, Lovewell! However, though you will not honour me with your confidence, I'll venture to truft you with mine.---What d'ye think of Mifs Sterling?

Lovew. What do I think of Mifs Sterling?

Sir John. Ay; what d'ye think of her?

Lovew. An odd queftion!--- but I think her a fmart, lively girl, full of mirth and fprightlinefs.

Sir John. All mifchief and malice, I doubt.

Lovew. How?

Sir John. But her perfon---what d'ye think of that?

Lovew. Pretty and agreeable.

Sir John. A little grifette thing.

Lovew. What is the meaning of all this?

Sir John. I'll tell you. You muft know, Lovewell, that notwithftanding all appearances--- [*feeing Lord* Ogleby, *&c.*] We are interrupted---When they are gone, I'll explain.

Enter Lord Ogleby, Sterling, *Mrs.* Heidelberg, *Mifs* Sterling, *and* Fanny.

Lord Ogle. Great improvements indeed, Mr. Sterling! wonderful improvements! The four feafons in lead, the flying Mercury, and the bafin with Neptune in the middle, are all in the very extreme of fine tafte. You have as many rich figures as the man at Hyde-Park Corner.

Sterl. The chief pleafure of a country houfe is to make improvements, you know, my Lord. I fpare no expence, not I.---This is quite another-guefs fort of a place than it was when I firft took it, my Lord. We were furrounded with trees. I cut down above fifty to make the lawn before the houfe, and let in the wind and the fun---fmack-fmooth---as you fee. ---Then I made a green-houfe out of the old laundry,

and

and turned the brew-houſe into a pinery.---The high octagon ſummer-houſe, you ſee yonder, is raiſed on the maſt of a ſhip, given me by an Eaſt-India captain, who has turned many a thouſand of my money. It commands the whole road. All the coaches and chariots, and chaiſes, paſs and repaſs under your eye. I'll mount you up there in the afternoon, my Lord. 'Tis the pleaſanteſt place in the world to take a pipe and a bottle,---and ſo you ſhall ſay, my Lord.

Lord Ogle. Ay---or a bowl of punch, or a can of flip, Mr. Sterling! for it looks like a cabin in the air.---If flying chairs were in uſe, the captain might make a voyage to the Indies in it ſtill, if he had but a fair wind.

Canton. Ha! ha! ha! ha!

Mrs. Heidel. My brother's a little comacal in his ideas, my Lord!---But you'll excuſe him.---I have a little gothick dairy, fitted up entirely in my own taſte. ---In the evening I ſhall hope for the honour of your Lordſhip's company to take a diſh of tea there, or a ſullabub warm from the cow.

Lord Ogle. I have every moment a freſh opportunity of admiring the elegance of Mrs. Heidelberg ---the very flower of delicacy, and cream of politeneſs.

Mrs. Heidel. O my Lord! ⎫
Lord Ogle. O Madam! ⎬ *leering at each other.*

Sterl. How d'ye like theſe cloſe walks, my Lord?

Lord Ogle. A moſt excellent ſerpentine! It forms a perfect maze, and winds like a true lover's knot.

Sterl. Ay---here's none of your ſtrait lines here--- but all taſte---zig-zag---crinkum-crankum---in and out---right and left---to and again---twiſting and turning like a worm, my Lord!

Lord Ogle. Admirably laid out indeed, Mr. Sterling! one can hardly ſee an inch beyond one's noſe any where in theſe walks.---You are a moſt excellent œconomiſt of your land, and make a little go a great way.---It lies together in as ſmall parcels as if it was

placed

placed in pots out at your window in Gracechurch-Street.

Canton. Ha! ha! ha! ha!

Lord Ogle. What d'ye laugh at, Canton?

Canton. Ah! que cette fimilitude eft drole! So clever what you fay, mi Lor!

Lord Ogle. [*to Fanny.*] You feem mightily engaged, Madam. What are thofe pretty hands fo bufily employed about?

Fanny. Only making up a nofegay, my Lord!—Will your Lordfhip do me the honour of accepting it? [*prefenting it.*

Lord Ogle. I'll wear it next my heart, Madam!—I fee the young creature doats on me! [*apart.*

Mifs Sterl. Lord, Sifter! you've loaded his Lordfhip with a bunch of flowers as big as the cook or the nurfe carry to town on Monday morning for a beaupot.—Will your Lordfhip give me leave to prefent you with this rofe and a fprig of fweet-briar?

Lord Ogle. The trueft Emblems of yourfelf, Madam! all fweetnefs and poignancy.—A little jealous, poor foul! [*apart.*

Sterl. Now, my Lord, if you pleafe, I'll carry you to fee my Ruins.

Mrs. Heidel. You'll abfolutely fatigue his Lordfhip with overwalking, Brother!

Lord Ogle. Not at all, Madam! We're in the garden of Eden, you know; in the region of perpetual fpring, youth, and beauty. [*leering at the women.*

Mrs. Heidel. Quite the man of qualaty, I perteft. [*apart.*

Canton. Take a my arm, my Lor!
　　　　　　[*Lord* Ogleby *leans on him.*

Sterl. I'll only fhew his Lordfhip my ruins, and the cafcade, and the Chinefe bridge, and then we'll go in to breakfaft.

Lord Ogle. Ruins, did you fay, Mr. Sterling?

Sterl. Ay, ruins, my Lord! and they are reckoned very fine ones too. You would think them ready to
tumble

tumble on your head. It has juft coft me a hundred and fifty pounds to put my ruins in thorough repair. —This way, if your Lordfhip pleafes.

Lord Ogle. [*going, ftops.*] What fteeple's that we fee yonder? the parifh-church, I fuppofe.

Sterl. Ha! ha! ha! that's admirable. It is no church at all, my Lord! it is a fpire that I have built againft a tree, a field or two off, to terminate the profpect. One muft always have a church, or an obelifk, or a fomething, to terminate the profpect, you know. That's a rule in tafte, my Lord!

Lord Ogle. Very ingenious, indeed! For my part, I defire no finer profpect, than this I fee before me. [*leering at the women.*]—Simple, yet varied; bounded, yet extenfive.—Get away, Canton! [*pufhing away Canton.*] I want no affiftance.—I'll walk with the ladies.

Sterl. This way, my Lord!

Lord Ogle. Lead on, Sir!—We young folks here will follow you.—Madam!—Mifs Sterling!—Mifs Fanny! I attend you.

[*Exit, after* Sterling, *gallanting the ladies.*

Canton. [*following.*] He is cock o'de game, ma foy! [*Exit.*

Manent Sir John Melvil, *and* Lovewell.

Sir John. At length, thank heaven, I have an opportunity to unbofom.—I know you are faithful, Lovewell, and flatter myfelf you would rejoice to ferve me.

Lovew. Be affured, you may depend on me.

Sir John. You muft know then, notwithftanding all appearances, that this treaty of marriage between Mifs Sterling and me will come to nothing.

Lovew. How!

Sir John. It will be no match, Lovewell.

Lovew. No match?

Sir John. No.

Lovew. You amaze me. What fhould prevent it?

Sir John. I.

Lovew.

Lovew. You! wherefore?

Sir John. I don't like her.

Lovew. Very plain indeed! I never fuppofed that you was extremely devoted to her from inclination, but thought you always confidered it as a matter of convenience, rather than affection.

Sir John. Very true. I came into the family with-out any impreffions on my mind—with an unimpaffioned indifference ready to receive one woman as foon as another. I looked upon love, ferious, fober love, as a chimæra, and marriage as a thing of courfe, as you know moft people do. But I, who was lately fo great an infidel in love, am now one of its fincereft votaries.—In fhort, my defection from Mifs Sterling proceeds from the violence of my attachment to another.

Lovew. Another! So! fo! here will be fine work. And pray who is fhe?

Sir John. Who is fhe! who can fhe be? but Fanny, the tender, amiable, engaging Fanny.

Lovew. Fanny! What Fanny?

Sir John. Fanny Sterling. Her fifter—Is not fhe an angel, Lovewell?

Lovew. Her fifter? Confufion!—You muft not think of it, Sir John.

Sir John. Not think of it? I can think of nothing elfe. Nay, tell me, Lovewell! was it poffible for me to be indulged in a perpetual intercourfe with two fuch objects as Fanny and her fifter, and not find my heart led by infenfible attraction towards her?—You feem confounded—Why don't you anfwer me?

Lovew. Indeed, Sir John, this event gives me infinite concern.

Sir John. Why fo?—Is not fhe an angel, Love-well?

Love. I forefee that it muft produce the worft confequences. Confider the confufion it muft una-voidably create. Let me perfuade you to drop thefe thoughts in time.

Sir

Sir John. Never—never, Lovewell!

Lovew. You have gone too far to recede. A negotiation, fo nearly concluded, cannot be broken off with any grace. The lawyers, you know, are hourly expected; the preliminaries almoſt finally ſettled between Lord Ogleby and Mr. Sterling; and Miſs Sterling herſelf ready to receive you as a huſband.

Sir John. Why the banns have been publiſhed, and nobody has forbidden them, 'tis true. But you know either of the parties may change their minds even after they enter the church.

Lovew. You think too lightly of this matter. To carry your addreſſes ſo far—and then to deſert her— and for her ſiſter too!—It will be ſuch an affront to the family, that they can never put up with it.

Sir John. I don't think ſo: for as to my transfer-ring my paſſion from her to her ſiſter, ſo much the better! for then, you know, I don't carry my af-fection out of the family.

Lovew. Nay, but prithee be ſerious, and think better of it.

Sir John. I have thought better of it already, you ſee. Tell me honeſtly, Lovewell! Can you blame me? Is there any compariſon between them?

Lovew. As to that now—why that—is juſt—juſt as it may ſtrike different people. There are many admirers of Miſs Sterling's vivacity.

Sir John. Vivacity! a medley of Cheapſide pert-neſs, and Whitechapel pride.—No—no, if I do go ſo far into the city for a wedding-dinner, it ſhall be upon turtle at leaſt.

Lovew. But I ſee no probability of ſucceſs; for granting that Mr. Sterling wou'd have conſented to it at firſt, he cannot liſten to it now. Why did not you break this affair to the family before?

Sir John. Under ſuch embarraſſed circumſtances as I have been, can you wonder at my irreſolution or perplexity? Nothing but deſpair, the fear of loſing my dear Fanny, cou'd bring me to a declaration

even

even now: and yet, I think, I know Mr. Sterling so well, that, strange as my proposal may appear, if I can make it advantageous to him as a money-transaction, as I am sure I can, he will certainly come into it.

Lovew. But even suppose he should, which I very much doubt, I don't think Fanny herself wou'd listen to your addresses.

Sir John. You are deceived a little in that particular.

Lovew. You'll find I am in the right.

Sir John. I have some little reason to think otherwise.

Lovew. You have not declared your passion to her already?

Sir John. Yes, I have.

Lovew. Indeed!—And—and—and how did she receive it?

Sir John. I think it is not very easy for me to make my addresses to any woman, without receiving some little encouragement.

Lovew. Encouragement! did she give you any encouragement?

Sir John. I don't know what you call encouragement—but she blushed—and cried—and desired me not to think of it any more:—upon which I prest her hand—kissed it—swore she was an angel—and I cou'd see it tickled her to the soul.

Lovew. And did she express no surprize at your declaration?

Sir John. Why, faith, to say the truth, she was a little surprized—and she got away from me too, before I cou'd thoroughly explain myself. If I should not meet with an opportunity of speaking to her, I must get you to deliver a letter from me.

Lovew. I!---a letter !---I had rather have nothing---

Sir John. Nay, you promised me your assistance---and I am sure you cannot scruple to make yourself useful on such an occasion.----You may, without suspicion,

D

picion, acquaint her verbally of my determined affection for her, and that I am resolved to ask her father's consent.

Lovew. As to that, I—your commands, you know—that is, if she—Indeed, Sir John, I think you are in the wrong.

Sir John. Well—well—that's my concern—Ha! there she goes, by heaven! along that walk yonder, d'ye see? I'll go to her immediately.

Lovew. You are too precipitate. Consider what you are doing.

Sir John. I wou'd not lose this opportunity for the universe.

Lovew. Nay, pray don't go! Your violence and eagerness may overcome her spirits.—The shock will be too much for her. [*detaining him.*

Sir John. Nothing shall prevent me.—Ha! now she turns into another walk.—Let me go! [*breaks from him.*] I shall lose her.—[*going, turns back.*] Be sure now to keep out of the way! If you interrupt us, I shall never forgive you. [*Exit hastily.*

Lovewell *alone.*

'Sdeath! I can't bear this. In love with my wife! acquaint me with his passion for her! make his addresses before my face!—I shall break out before my time.—This was the meaning of Fanny's uneasiness. She could not encourage him.—I am sure she could not.—Ha! they are turning into the walk, and coming this way. Shall I leave the place?—Leave him to solicit my wife! I can't submit to it.—They come nearer and nearer—If I stay, it will look suspicious—It may betray us, and incense him—They are here—I must go—I am the most unfortunate fellow in the world. [*Exit.*

Enter Fanny, *and Sir* John.

Fanny. Leave me, Sir John, I beseech you leave me—nay, why will you persist to follow me with
idle

idle folicitations, which are an affront to my character, and an injury to your own honour?

Sir John. I know your delicacy, and tremble to offend it: but let the urgency of the occafion be my excufe! Confider, Madam, that the future happinefs of my life depends on my prefent application to you! confider that this day muft determine my fate; and thefe are perhaps the only moments left me to incline you to warrant my paffion, and to intreat you not to oppofe the propofals I mean to open to your father.

Fanny. For fhame, for fhame, Sir John! Think of your previous engagements! Think of your own fituation, and think of mine!—What have you difcovered in my conduct that might encourage you to fo bold a declaration? I am fhocked that you fhould venture to fay fo much, and blufh that I fhould even dare to give it a hearing.—Let me be gone!

Sir John. Nay, ftay, Madam! but one moment—Your fenfibility is too great.—Engagements! what engagements have even been pretended on either fide than thofe of family-convenience? I went on in the trammels of matrimonial negotiation with a blind fubmiffion to your father and Lord Ogleby; but my heart foon claimed a right to be confulted. It has devoted itfelf to you, and obliges me to plead earneftly for the fame tender intereft in yours.

Fanny. Have a care, Sir John! do not miftake a depraved will for a virtuous inclination. By thefe common pretences of the heart, half of our fex are made fools, and a greater part of yours defpife them for it.

Sir John. Affection, you will allow, is involuntary. We cannot always direct it to the object on which it fhould fix—But when it is once inviolably attached, inviolably as mine is to you, it often creates reciprocal affection.—When I laft urged you on this fubject, you heard me with more temper, and I hoped with fome compaffion.

Fanny.

Fanny. You deceived yourself. If I forbore to exert a proper spirit, nay if I did not even exprefs the quickest refentment of your behaviour, it was only in confideration of that refpect I wish to pay you, in honour to my fifter: and be affured, Sir, woman as I am, that my vanity could reap no pleafure from a triumph, that muft refult from the blackeft treachery to her.   [*going.*

Sir John. One word, and I have done. [*ftopping her.*]—Your impatience and anxiety, and the urgency of the occafion, oblige me to be brief and explicit with you.—I appeal therefore from your delicacy to your juftice.—Your fifter, I verily believe, neither entertains any real affection for me, or tendernefs for you.—Your father, I am inclined to think, is not much concerned by means of which of his daughters the families are united.—Now as they cannot, fhall not be connected, otherwise than by my union with you, why will you, from a falfe delicacy, oppofe a meafure fo conducive to my happinefs, and, I hope, your own?—I love you, moft paffionately and fincerely love you—and hope to propofe terms agreeable to Mr. Sterling.—If then you don't abfolutely loath, abhor, and fcorn me—if there is no other happier man——

Fanny. Hear me, Sir, hear my final determination—Were my father and fifter as infenfible as you are pleafed to reprefent them;—were my heart for ever to remain difengaged to any other—I could not liften to your propofals—What! You on the very eve of a marriage with my fifter; I living under the fame roof with her, bound not only by the laws of friendfhip and hofpitality, but even the ties of blood, to contribute to her happinefs,—and not to confpire againft her peace—the peace of a whole family—and that my own too!—Away! away, Sir John!—At fuch a time, and in fuch circumftances, your addreffes only infpire me with horror.---Nay, you muft detain me no longer.---I will go.

Sir

Sir John. Do not leave me in abfolute defpair!---
Give me a glimpfe of hope! [*falling on his knees.*]

Fanny. I cannot. Pray, Sir John! [*ftruggling to go.*]

Sir John. Shall this hand be given to another?
[*kiffing her hand.*] No---I cannot endure it.---My
whole foul is yours, and the whole happinefs of my
life is in your power.

Enter Mifs Sterling.

Fanny. Ha! my fifter is here. Rife for fhame,
Sir John!

Sir John. Mifs Sterling! [*rifing.*]

Mifs Sterl. I beg pardon, Sir!---You'll excufe me,
Madam!---I have broke in upon you a little unoppor-
tunely, I believe---But I did not mean to interrupt
you---I only came, Sir, to let you know that breakfaft waits, if you have finifhed your morning's devo-
tions.

Sir John. I am very fenfible, Mifs Sterling, that
this may appear particular, but——

Mifs Sterl. O dear, Sir John, don't put yourfelf
to the trouble of an apology. The thing explains
itfelf.

Sir John. It will foon, Madam!---In the mean
time, I can only affure you of my profound refpect
and efteem for you, and make no doubt of convincing
Mr. Sterling of the honour and integrity of my
intentions. And---and---your humble fervant, Madam! [*Exit in confufion.*]

Manent Fanny, *and Mifs* Sterling.

Mifs Sterl. Refpect?---Infolence!---Efteem?---Very
fine truly!---And you, Madam! my fweet, delicate,
innocent, fentimental fifter! will you convince my
papa too of the integrity of your intentions?

Fanny. Do not upbraid me, my dear fifter! Indeed,
I don't deferve it. Believe me, you can't be more
offended at his behaviour than I am, and I am fure
it cannot make you half fo miferable.

D 3

Miss Sterl. Make me miferable! You are mightily deceived, Madam! It gives me no fort of uneafinefs, I affure you.---A bafe fellow!---As for you, Mifs! the pretended foftnefs of your difpofition, your artful good-nature, never impofed upon me. I always knew you to be fly, and envious, and deceitful.

Fanny. Indeed you wrong me.

Miss Sterl. Oh, you are all goodnefs, to be fure! ---Did not I find him on his knees before you? Did not I fee him kifs your fweet hand? Did not I hear his proteftations? Was not I witnefs of your dif-fembled modefty?---No---no, my dear! don't imagine that you can make a fool of your elder fifter fo eafily.

Fanny. Sir John, I own, is to blame; but I am above the thoughts of doing you the leaft injury.

Miss. Sterl. We fhall try that, Madam!---I hope, Mifs, you'll be able to give a better account to my papa and my aunt---for they fhall both know of this matter, I promife you.   [*Exit.*

Fanny *alone.*

How unhappy I am! my diftreffes multiply upon me.---Mr. Lovewell muft now become acquainted with Sir John's behaviour to me, and in a manner that may add to his uneafinefs.---My father, inftead of being difpofed by fortunate circumftances to for-give any tranfgreffion, will be previoufly incenfed againft me. My fifter and my aunt will become irreconcilably my enemies, and rejoice in my difgrace. ---Yet, on all events, I am determined on a difcovery. I dread it, and am refolved to haften it. It is fur-rounded with more horrors every inftant, as it ap-pears every inftant more neceffary.   [*Exit.*

ACT

ACT III. SCENE I.

A hall.

Enter a servant leading in Serjeant Flower, *and Coun-
sellors* Traverse *and* Trueman---*all booted.*

Servant. THIS way, if you please, gentlemen!
my master is at breakfast with the fa-
mily at present---but I'll let him know, and he will
wait on you immediately.

Flower. Mighty well, young man, mighty well.

Servant. Please to favour me with your names.

Flower. Let Mr. Sterling know, that Mr. Serjeant
Flower, and two other gentlemen of the bar, are
come to wait on him according to his appointment.

Servant. I will, Sir. [*going.*

Flower. And harkee, young man! [*servant returns.*] Desire my servant---Mr. Serjeant Flower's
servant---to bring in my green and gold saddle-cloth
and pistols, and lay them down here in the hall with
my portmanteau.

Servant. I will, Sir. [*Exit.*

Manent Lawyers.

Flower. Well, gentlemen! the settling these marriage articles falls conveniently enough, almost just
on the eve of the circuits.---Let me see---the Home,
the Midland, and Western,---ay, we can all cross the
country well enough to our several destinations.---
Traverse, when do you begin at Hertford?

Traverse. The day after to-morrow.

Flower. That is a commission-day with us at Warwick too.---But my clerk has retainers for every
cause in the paper, so it will be time enough if I
am there the next morning.---Besides, I have about
half a dozen cases that have lain by me ever since
the spring assizes, and I must tack opinions to them

D 4 before

before I see my country clients again—so I will take the evening before me—and then *currente calamo*, as I say---eh, Traverse!

Traverse. True, Mr. Serjeant — and the easiest thing in the world too—for those country attornies are such ignorant dogs, that in case of the devise of an estate to A. and his heirs for ever, they'll make a query, whether he takes in fee or in tail.

Flower. Do you expect to have much to do on the Home circuit these assizes?

Traverse. Not much *nisi prius* business, but a good deal on the crown side, I believe.—The gaols are brimfull—and some of the felons in good circumstances, and likely to be tolerable clients.—Let me see! I am engaged for three highway robberies, two murders, one forgery, and half a dozen larcenies, at Kingston.

Flower. A pretty decent gaol-delivery!—Do you expect to bring off Darkin, for the robbery on Putney-Common? Can you make out your *alibi?*

Traverse. Oh no! the crown witnesses are sure to prove our identity. We shall certainly be hanged: but that don't signify.—But, Mr. Serjeant, have you much to do?—any remarkable cause on the Midland this circuit?

Flower. Nothing very remarkable,—except two rapes, and Rider and Western at Nottingham, for *crim. con.*—but, on the whole, I believe a good deal of business.---Our associate tells me, there are above thirty *venires* for Warwick.

Traverse. Pray, Mr. Serjeant, are you concerned in Jones and Thomas at Lincoln?

Flower. I am—for the plaintiff.

Traverse. And what do you think on't?

Flower. A nonsuit.

Traverse. I thought so.

Flower. Oh, no manner of doubt on't—*luce clarius,*—we have no right in us—we have but one chance.

Tra-

Traverse. What's that?

Flower. Why, my Lord Chief does not go the circuit this time, and my brother Puzzle being in the commiffion, the caufe will come on before him.

Trueman. Ay, that may do, indeed, if you can but throw duft in the eyes of the defendant's counfel.

Flower. True.—Mr. Trueman, I think you are concerned for Lord Ogleby in this affair? [*to* Trueman.

Trueman. I am, Sir—I have the honour to be related to his Lordfhip, and hold fome courts for him in Somerfetfhire—go the Weftern circuit—and attend the feffions at Exeter, merely becaufe his Lordfhip's intereft and property lie in that part of the kingdom.

Flower. Ha!—and pray, Mr. Trueman, how long have you been called to the bar?

Trueman. About nine years and three quarters.

Flower. Ha!—I don't know that I ever had the pleafure of feeing you before.—I wifh you fuccefs, young gentleman!

Enter Sterling.

Sterl. Oh, Mr. Serjeant Flower, I am glad to fee you—Your fervant, Mr. Serjeant! gentlemen, your fervant!—Well, are all matters concluded? Has that fnail-paced conveyancer, old Ferret of Gray's Inn, fettled the articles at laft? Do you approve of what he has done? Will his tackle hold? tight and ftrong?—Eh, mafter Serjeant?

Flower. My friend Ferret's flow and fure, Sir—But then, *ferius aut citius*, we fay,—fooner or later, Mr. Sterling, he is fure to put his bufinefs out of hand as he fhould do.—My clerk has brought the writings, and all other inftruments along with him, and the fettlement is, I believe, as good a fettlement as any fettlement on the face of the earth!

Sterl. But that damn'd mortgage of 60,000 *l.*—There don't appear to be any other incumbrances, I hope?

Tra-

Traverfe. I can anfwer for that, Sir—and that will be cleared off immediately on the payment of the firft part of Mifs Sterling's portion.—You agree, on your part, to come down with 80,000*l.*—

Sterl. Down on the nail.—Ay, ay, my money is ready to-morrow if he pleafes—he fhall have it in India bonds, or notes, or how he chufes.—Your lords, and your dukes, and your people at the court-end of the town ftick at payments fometimes—debts unpaid, no credit loft with them—but no fear of us fubftantial fellows—eh, Mr. Serjeant!—

Flower. Sir John having laft term, according to agreement, levied a fine, and fuffered a recovery, has thereby cut off the entail of the Ogleby eftate for the better effecting the purpofes of the prefent intended marriage; on which above-mentioned Ogleby eftate, a jointure of 2000*l. per ann.* is fecured to your eldeft daughter, now Elizabeth Sterling, fpinfter, and the whole eftate, after the death of the aforefaid Earl, defcends to the heirs male of Sir John Melvil, on the body of the aforefaid Elizabeth Sterling lawfully to be begotten.

Traverfe. Very true—and Sir John is to be put in immediate poffeffion of as much of his Lordfhip's Somerfetfhire eftate, as lies in the manors of Hogmore and Cranford, amounting to between two and three thoufand *per ann.* and at the death of Mr. Sterling, a further fum of feventy thoufand——

Enter *Sir* John Melvil.

Sterl. Ah, Sir John! Here we are—hard at it—paving the road to matrimony—Firft the lawyers, then comes the doctor—Let us but difpatch the long-robe, we fhall foon get pudding-fleeves to work, I warrant you.

Sir John. I am forry to interrupt you, Sir—but I hope that both you and thefe gentlemen will excufe me—having fomething very particular for your private ear, I took the liberty of following you, and

beg

beg you will oblige me with an audience immediately.

Sterl. Ay, with all my heart!—Gentlemen, Mr. Serjeant, you'll excuse it—Business must be done, you know.—The writings will keep cold till to-morrow morning.

Flower. I must be at Warwick, Mr. Sterling, the day after.

Sterl. Nay, nay, I shan't part with you to-night, gentlemen, I promise you.—My house is very full, but I have beds for you all, beds for your servants, and stabling for all your horses.—Will you take a turn in the garden, and view some of my improvements before dinner? Or will you amuse yourselves on the green with a game of bowls and a cool tankard?—My servants shall attend you—Do you chuse any other refreshment?—Call for what you please;—do as you please;—make yourselves quite at home, I beg of you.—Here,—Thomas! Harry! William! wait on these gentlemen!—[*follows the lawyers out, bawling and talking, and then returns to Sir John.*] And now, Sir, I am entirely at your service.—What are your commands with me, Sir John?

Sir John. After having carried the negotiation between our families to so great a length, after having assented so readily to all your proposals, as well as received so many instances of your chearful compliance with the demands made on our part, I am extremely concerned, Mr. Sterling, to be the involuntary cause of any uneasiness.

Sterl. Uneasiness! what uneasiness!—Where business is transacted as it ought to be, and the parties understand one another, there can be no uneasiness. You agree, on such and such conditions, to receive my daughter for a wife; on the same conditions I agree to receive you as a son-in-law; and as to all the rest, it follows of course, you know, as regularly as the payment of a bill after acceptance.

Sir

Sir John. Pardon me, Sir; more uneasiness has arisen than you are aware of. I am myself, at this instant, in a state of inexpressible embarrassment; Miss Sterling, I know, is extremely disconcerted too; and unless you will oblige me with the assistance of your friendship, I foresee the speedy progress of discontent and animosity through the whole family.

Sterl. What the deuce is all this? I don't understand a single syllable.

Sir John. In one word then—it will be absolutely impossible for me to fulfil my engagements in regard to Miss Sterling.

Sterl. How, Sir John! Do you mean to put an affront upon my family? What! refuse to—

Sir John. Be assured, Sir, that I neither mean to affront, nor forsake your family.—My only fear is, that you should desert me; for the whole happiness of my life depends on my being connected with your family by the nearest and tenderest ties in the world.

Sterl. Why, did not you tell me, but a moment ago, that it was absolutely impossible for you to marry my daughter?

Sir John. True.—But you have another daughter, Sir——

Sterl. Well!

Sir John. Who has obtained the most absolute dominion over my heart. I have already declared my passion to her; nay, Miss Sterling herself is also apprized of it, and if you will but give a sanction to my present addresses, the uncommon merit of Miss Sterling will no doubt recommend her to a person of equal, if not superior rank to myself, and our families may still be allied by my union with Miss Fanny.

Sterl. Mighty fine, truly! Why, what the plague do you make of us, Sir John? Do you come to market for my daughter, like servants at a statute-fair? Do you think that I will suffer you, or any man in the world, to come into my house, like the

Grand

Grand Signior, and throw the handkerchief first to one, and then to t'other; just as he pleases? Do you think I drive a kind of African slave-trade with them?, and——

Sir John. A moment's patience, Sir! Nothing but the excess of my passion for Miss Fanny shou'd have induced me to take any step that had the least appearance of any disrespect to any part of your family; and even now I am desirous to atone for my transgression, by making the most adequate compensation that lies in my power.

Sterl. Compensation! what compensation can you possibly make in such a case as this, Sir John?

Sir John. Come, come, Mr. Sterling; I know you to be a man of sense, a man of business, a man of the world. I'll deal frankly with you; and you shall see that I don't desire a change of measures for my own gratification, without endeavouring to make it advantageous to you.

Sterl. What advantage can your inconstancy be to me, Sir John?

Sir John. I'll tell you, Sir.—You know that by the articles at present subsisting between us, on the day of my marriage with Miss Sterling, you agree to pay down the gross sum of eighty thousand pounds.

Sterl. Well!

Sir John. Now if you will but consent to my waving that marriage——

Sterl. I agree to your waving that marriage? Impossible, Sir John!

Sir John. I hope not, Sir; as on my part, I will agree to wave my right to thirty thousand pounds of the fortune I was to receive with her.

Sterl. Thirty thousand, d'ye say?

Sir John. Yes, Sir; and accept of Miss Fanny with fifty thousand, instead of fourscore.

Sterl. Fifty thousand——   [*pausing.*

Sir John. Instead of fourscore.

Sterl.

Sterl. Why,—why,—there may be fomething in that.—Let me fee ; Fanny with fifty thoufand inftead of Betfey with fourfcore—But how can this be, Sir John ?—For you know I am to pay this money into the hands of my Lord Ogleby ; who, I believe— between you and me, Sir John,—is not overftocked with ready money at prefent ; and threefcore thou- fand of it, you know, is to go to pay off the prefent incumbrances on the eftate, Sir John.

Sir John. That objection is eafily obviated.—Ten of the twenty. thoufand, which would remain as a furplus of the fourfcore, after paying off the mort- gage, was intended by his Lordfhip for my ufe, that we might fet off with fome little *eclat* on our mar- riage ; and the other ten for his own.—Ten thoufand pounds, therefore, I fhall be able to pay you imme- diately ; and for the remaining twenty thoufand, you fhall have a mortgage on that part of the eftate which is to be made over to me, with whatever fecurity you fhall require for the regular payment of the intereft, till the principal is duly difcharged.

Sterl. Why—to do you juftice, Sir John, there is fomething fair and open in your propofal ; and fince I find you do not mean to put an affront upon the family——

Sir John. Nothing was ever farther from my thoughts, Mr. Sterling.—And after all, the whole affair is nothing extraordinary—fuch things happen every day—and as the world has only heard generally of a treaty between the families, when this marriage takes place, nobody will be the wifer, if we have but difcretion enough to keep our own counfel.

Sterl. True, true ; and fince you only transfer from one girl to the other, it is no more than transferring fo much ftock, you know.

Sir John. The very thing.

Sterl. Odfo ! I had quite forgot. We are reckon- ing without our hoft here. There is another diffi- culty—

5

Sir

Sir John. You alarm me. What can that be?

Sterl. I can't stir a step in this busineſs without conſulting my ſiſter Heidelberg.—The family has very great expectations from her, and we muſt not give her any offence.

Sir John. But if you come into this meaſure, ſurely ſhe will be ſo kind as to conſent—

Sterl. I don't know that—Betſey is her darling, and I can't tell how far ſhe may reſent any ſlight that ſeems to be offered to her favourite niece.—However, I'll do the beſt I can for you.—You ſhall go and break the matter to her firſt, and by that time that I may ſuppoſe that your rhetoric has prevailed on her to liſten to reaſon, I will ſtep in to reinforce your arguments.

Sir John. I'll fly to her immediately : you promiſe me your aſſiſtance ?

Sterl. I do.

Sir John. Ten thouſand thanks for it ! and now ſucceſs attend me !   [*going.*

Sterl. Harkee, Sir John !

Sir John *returns.*

Sterl. Not a word of the thirty thouſand to my ſiſter, Sir John.

Sir John. Oh, I am dumb, I am dumb, Sir,
                                                      [*going.*

Sterl. You remember it is thirty thouſand.

Sir John. To be ſure I do.

Sterl. But Sir John !—one thing more. [*Sir* John *returns.*] My Lord muſt know nothing of this ſtroke of friendſhip between us.

Sir John. Not for the world.—Let me alone ! let me alone !   [*offering to go.*

Sterl. [*holding him.*]—And when every thing is agreed, we muſt give each other a bond to be held faſt to the bargain.

Sir John. To be ſure. A bond by all means ! a bond, or whatever you pleaſe.   [*Exit haſtily.*

Sterling

Sterling *alone.*

I fhould have thought of more conditions—he's in a humour to give me every thing—Why, what mere children are your fellows of quality; that cry for a play-thing one minute, and throw it by the next! as changeable as the weather, and as uncertain as the ftocks.—Special fellows to drive a bargain! and yet they are to take care of the intereft of the nation, truly!—Here does this whirligig man of fafhion offer to give up thirty thoufand pounds in hard money, with as much indifference as if it was a china-orange.—By this mortgage, I fhall have a hold on his *Terra-firma,* and if he wants more money, as he certainly will,—let him have children by my daughter or no, I fhall have his whole eftate in a net for the benefit of my family.—Well; thus it is, that the children of citizens, who have acquired fortunes, prove perfons of fafhion; and thus it is, that perfons of fafhion, who have ruined their fortunes, reduce the next generation to cits.   [*Exit.*

SCENE *changes to another apartment.*

Enter Mrs. Heidelberg, *and Mifs* Sterling.

Mifs Sterl. This is your gentle-looking, foft-fpeaking, fweet-fmiling, affable Mifs Fanny for you!

Mrs. Heidel. My Mifs Fanny! I difclaim her. With all her arts fhe never could infinuate herfelf into my good graces—and yet fhe has a way with her, that deceives man, woman, and child, except you and me, niece.

Mifs Sterl. O ay; fhe wants nothing but a crook in her hand, and a lamb under her arm, to be a perfect picture of innocence and fimplicity.

Mrs. Heidel. Juft as I was drawn at Amfterdam, when I went over to vifit my hufband's relations.

Mifs Sterl. And then fhe's fo mighty good to fervants—pray, *John, do this*—pray, *Tom, do that*—thank

you,

you, Jenny—and then so humble to her relations—*to be sure, Papa!*—*as my Aunt pleases*—*my Sister knows best*—But with all her demureness and humility she has no objection to be Lady Melvil, it seems, nor to any wickedness that can make her so.

Mrs. Heidel. She Lady Melville? Compose your-self, niece! I'll ladyship her indeed :—a little crep-pin, cantin—She shan't be the better for a farden of my money. But tell me, child, how does this in-triguing with Sir John correspond with her partiality to Lovewell? I don't see a concatunation here.

Miss Sterl. There I was deceived, Madam. I took all their whisperings and stealing into corners to be the mere attraction of vulgar minds ; but, behold ! their private meetings were not to contrive their own insipid happiness, but to conspire against mine.—But I know whence proceeds Mr. Lovewell's resentment to me. I could not stoop to be familiar with my fa-ther's clerk, and so I have lost his interest.

Mrs. Heidel. My spurrit to a T.—my dear child ! [*kissing her.*]—Mr. Heidelberg lost his election for member of parliament, because I would not demean myself to be slobbered about by drunken shoemakers, beastly cheesemongers, and greasy butchers and tallow-chandlers. However, niece, I can't help dif-furring a little in opinion from you in this matter. My experunce and sagucity makes me still suspect, that there is something more between her and that Lovewell, notwithstanding this affair of Sir John.—I had my eye upon them the whole time of break-fast.—Sir John, I observed, looked a little confound-ed, indeed, though I knew nothing of what had passed in the garden. You seemed to sit upon thorns too: But Fanny and Mr. Lovewell made quite ano-ther-guess sort of a figur ; and were as perfect a pictur of two distrest lovers, as if it had been drawn by Raphael Angelo.—As to Sir John and Fanny, I want a matter of fact.

E   *Miss*

Miſs Sterl. Matter of fact, Madam? Did not I come unexpectedly upon them? Was not Sir John kneeling at her feet, and kiſſing her hands? Did not he look all love, and ſhe all confuſion? Is not that matter of fact? And did not Sir John, the moment that Papa was called out of the room to the lawyer-men, get up from breakfaſt, and follow him imme-diately? And I warrant you that by this time he has made propoſals to him to marry my ſiſter—Oh, that ſome other perſon, an earl, or a duke, would make his addreſſes to me, that I might be revenged on this monſter!

Mrs. Heidel. Be cool, child! you *ſhall* be Lady Melvil, in ſpite of all their caballins, if it coſts me ten thouſand pounds to turn the ſcale. Sir John may apply to my brother, indeed; but I'll make them all know who governs in this fammaly.

Miſs Sterl. As I live, Madam, yonder comes Sir John. A baſe man! I can't endure the ſight of him. I'll leave the room this inſtant. [*diſordered.*

Mrs. Heidel. Poor thing! Well, retire to your own chamber, child; I'll give it him, I warrant you; and by and by I'll come and let you know all that has paſt between us.

Miſs Sterl. Pray do, Madam!—[*looking back.*]— A vile wretch! [*Exit in a rage.*

Enter Sir John Melvil.

Sir John. Your moſt obedient humble ſervant, Madam! [*bowing very reſpectfully.*

Mrs. Heidel. Your ſervant, Sir John!
[*dropping a half-curtſey, and pouting.*

Sir John. Miſs Sterling's manner of quitting the room on my approach, and the viſible coolneſs of your behaviour to me, Madam, convince me that ſhe has acquainted you with what paſt this morning.

Mrs. Heidel. I am very ſorry, Sir John, to be made acquainted with any thing that ſhould induce me to change the opinion, which I could always wiſh to entertain of a perſon of qualaty. [*pouting.*

Sir

Sir John. It has always been my ambition to merit the beft opinion from Mrs. Heidelberg; and when fhe comes to weigh all circumftances, I flatter my-felf——

Mrs. Heidel. You *do* flatter yourfelf, if you ima-gine that I can approve of your behaviour to my niece, Sir John.—And give me leave to tell you, Sir John, that you have been drawn into an action much beneath you, Sir John; and that I look upon every injury offered to Mifs Betty Sterling, as an affront to myfelf, Sir John.   [*warmly.*

Sir John. I would not offend you for the world, Madam! but when I am influenced by a partiality for another, however ill-founded, I hope your dif-cernment and good fenfe will think it rather a point of honour to renounce engagements, which I could not fulfil fo ftrictly as I ought; and that you will excufe the change in my inclinations, fince the new object, as well as the firft, has the honour of being your niece, Madam.

Mrs. Heidel. I difclaim her as a niece, Sir John; Mifs Sterling difclaims her as a fifter, and the whole fammaly muft difclaim her, for her monftrous bafe-nefs and treachery.

Sir John. Indeed fhe has been guilty of none, Madam. Her hand and heart are, I am fure, en-tirely at the difpofal of yourfelf, and Mr. Sterling.

                    Enter Sterling *behind.*

And if you fhould not oppofe my inclinations, I am fure of Mr. Sterling's confent, Madam.

Mrs. Heidel. Indeed!

Sir John. Quite certain, Madam.

Sterl. [*behind.*] So! they feem to be coming to terms already. I may venture to make my ap-pearance.

Mrs. Heidel. To marry Fanny?

                    [Sterling *advances by degrees.*

Sir John. Yes, Madam.

Mrs. Heidel. My brother has given his confent, you fay?   E 2 .   *Sir*

Sir John. In the moſt ample manner, with no other reſtriction than the failure of your concurrence, Madam.—[*ſees* Sterling.]—Oh, here's Mr. Sterling, who will confirm what I have told you.

Mrs. Heidel. What! have you conſented to give up your own daughter in this manner, brother?

Sterl. Give her up! no, not give her up, ſiſter; only in caſe that you—Zounds, I am afraid you have ſaid too much, Sir John.   [*apart to Sir* John.

Mrs. Heidel. Yes, yes. I ſee now that it is true enough what my niece told me. You are all plottin and caballin againſt her. — Pray, does Lord Ogleby know of this affair?

Sir John. I have not yet made him acquainted with it, Madam.

Mrs. Heidel. No, I warrant you. I thought ſo. —And ſo his Lordſhip and myſelf truly, are not to be conſulted 'till the laſt.

Sterl. What! did not you conſult my Lord? Oh, fie for ſhame, Sir John!

Sir John. Nay, but Mr. Sterling—

Mrs. Heidel. We, who are the perſons of moſt conſequence and experunce in the two fammalies, are to know nothing of the matter, 'till the whole is as good as concluded upon. But his Lordſhip, I am ſure, will have more generoſaty than to countenance ſuch a perceding.—And I could not have expected ſuch behaviour from a perſon of your quallaty, Sir John—And as for you, brother—

Sterl. Nay, nay, but hear me, ſiſter!

Mrs. Heidel. I am perfectly aſhamed of you— Have you no ſpurrit? no more concern for the honour of our fammaly than to conſent—

Sterl. Conſent?—I conſent?—As I hope for mercy, I never gave my conſent. Did I conſent, Sir John?

Sir John. Not abſolutely, without Mrs. Heidelberg's concurrence. But in caſe of her approbation—

Sterl.

Sterl. Ay, I grant you, if my fifter approved—
But that's quite another thing, you know—
[*to Mrs.* Heidelberg.

Mrs. Heidel. Your fifter approve, indeed!—I
thought you knew her better, brother Sterling!—
What! approve of having your eldeft daughter re-
turned upon your hands, and exchanged for the
younger?—I am furprized how you could liften to
fuch a fcandalus propofal.

Sterl. I tell you, I never did liften to it.—Did not
I fay that I would be governed entirely by my fifter,
Sir John!—And unlefs fhe agreed to your marrying
Fanny—

Mrs. Heidel. I agree to his marrying Fanny?
abominable! The man is abfolutely out of his fenfes.
—Can't that wife head of yours forefee the confequence of all this, brother Sterling? Will Sir John
take Fanny without a fortin!—No.—After you have
fettled the largeft part of your property on your
youngeft daughter, can there be an equal portion
left for the eldeft? No.—Does not this overturn the
whole fyftum of the fammaly? Yes, yes, yes. You
know I was always for my niece Betfey's marrying
a perfon of the very firft quallaty. That was my
maxum. And, therefore, much the largeft fettlement was of courfe to be made upon her.—As for
Fanny, if fhe could, with a fortune of twenty or
thirty thoufand pounds, get a knight, or a member
of parliament, or a rich common-council-man for a
hufband, I thought it might do very well.

Sir John. But if a better match fhould offer itfelf,
why fhould not it be accepted, Madam?

Mrs. Heidel. What at the expence of her elder
fifter! O fie, Sir John! How could you bear to
hear of fuch an indignaty, brother Sterling!

Sterl. I! Nay, I fhan't hear of it I promife you,—
I can't hear of it indeed, Sir John.

Mrs. Heidel. But you *have* heard of it, brother
Sterling. You know you have; and fent Sir John

to propofe it to me. But if you can give up your daughter, I fhan't forfake my niece, I affure you. Ah! if my poor dear Mr. Heidelberg and our fweet babes had been alive, he would not have behaved fo.

Sterl. Did I, Sir John? nay fpeak!---Bring me off, or we are ruined.   [*apart to Sir* John.

Sir John. Why to be fure, to fpeak the truth---

Mrs. Heidel. To fpeak the truth, I'm afhamed of you both. But have a care what you are about, brother! have a care, I fay. The counfellors are in the houfe, I hear; and if every thing is not fettled to my liking, I'll have nothing more to fay to you, if I live thefe hundred years---I'll go over to Holland, and fettle with Mr. Vanderfpracken, my poor hufband's firft coufin, and my own fammaly fhall never be the better for a farden of my money, I promife you.   [*Exit.*

Manent Sir John *and* Sterling.

Sterl. I thought fo. I knew fhe never would agree to it.

Sir John. 'Sdeath, how unfortunate! What can we do, Mr. Sterling?

Sterl. Nothing.

Sir John. What muft our agreement break off, the moment it is made then?

Sterl. It can't be helped, Sir John. The family, as I told you before, have great expectations from my fifter; and if this matter proceeds, you hear yourfelf that fhe threatens to leave us.---My brother Heidelberg was a warm man; a very warm man; and died worth a Plumb at leaft; a Plumb! ay, I warrant you, he died worth a Plumb and a half.

Sir John. Well; but if I---

Sterl. And then, my fifter has three or four very good mortgages, a deal of money in the three per cents. and old South-Sea annuities, befides large concerns in the Dutch and French funds.---The

greateft

greateſt part of all this ſhe means to leave to our family.

Sir John. I can only ſay, Sir---

Sterl. Why, your offer of the difference of thirty thouſand, was very fair and handſome, to be ſure, Sir John.

Sir John. Nay, but I am even willing to---

Sterl. Ay, but if I was to accept it againſt her will, I might loſe above a hundred thouſand; ſo you ſee the balance is againſt you, Sir John.

Sir John. But is there no way, do you think, of prevailing on Mrs. Heidelberg to grant her conſent?

Sterl. I am afraid not.---However, when her paſſion is a little abated---for ſhe's very paſſionate---you may try what can be done: but you muſt not uſe my name any more, Sir John.

Sir John. Suppoſe I was to prevail on Lord Ogleby to apply to her, do you think that would have any influence over her?

Sterl. I think he would be more likely to perſuade her to it than any other perſon in the family. She has a great reſpect for Lord Ogleby. She loves a lord.

Sir John. I'll apply to him this very day.---And if he ſhould prevail on Mrs. Heidelberg, I may depend on your friendſhip, Mr. Sterling?

Sterl. Ay, ay, I ſhall be glad to oblige you, when it is in my power; but as the account ſtands now, you ſee it is not upon the figures. And ſo your ſervant, Sir John,   [*Exit.*

Sir John Melvil *alone.*

What a ſituation am I in!---Breaking off with her whom I was bound by treaty to marry; rejected by the object of my affections; and embroiled with this turbulent woman, who governs the whole family.--- And yet oppoſition, inſtead of ſmothering, increaſes my inclination. I muſt have her. I'll apply imme-. diately to Lord Ogleby; and if he can but bring

over

over the aunt to our party, her influence will overcome the scruples and delicacy of my dear Fanny, and I shall be the happiest of mankind. [*Exit.*

ACT IV. SCENE I.

A room.

Enter Sterling, *Mrs.* Heidelberg, *and Miss* Sterling.

Sterl. WHAT! will you send Fanny to town, sister?

Mrs. Heidel. To-morrow morning. I've given orders about it already.

Sterl. Indeed?

Mrs. Heidel. Posatively.

Sterl. But consider, siste., at such a time as this, what an odd appearance it will have.

Mrs. Heidel. Not half so odd as her behaviour, brother.---This time was intended for happiness, and I'll keep no incendaries here to destroy it. I insist on her going off to-morrow morning.

Sterl. I'm afraid this is all your doing, Betsey.

Miss Sterl. No, indeed, Papa. My aunt knows that it is not.---For all Fanny's baseness to me, I am sure I would not do, or say any thing to hurt her with you or my aunt for the world.

Mrs. Heidel. Hold your tongue, Betsey!---I will have my way.---When she is packed off, every thing will go on as it should do.---Since they are at their intrigues, I'll let them see that we can act with vigur on our part; and the sending her out of the way shall be the purlimunary step to all the rest of my perceedings.

Sterl. Well, but sister---

Mrs. Heidel. It does not signify talking, brother Sterling, for I'm resolved to be rid of her, and I will.

---Come

---Come along, child! [*to Miss* Sterling.]---The post-
shay shall be at the door by six o'clock in the morning; and if Miss Fanny does not get into it, why I
will, and so there's an end of the matter.

[*bounces out with Miss* Sterling.

Mrs. Heidelberg *returns.*

Mrs. Heidel. One word more, brother Sterling !---
I expect that you will take your eldest daughter in
your hand, and make a formal complaint to Lord
Ogleby of Sir John Melvil's behaviour.---Do this,
brother; shew a proper regard for the honour of
your fammaly yourself, and I shall throw in my mite
to the raising of it. If not---but now you know my
mind. So act as you please, and take the conse-
quences. [*Exit.*

Sterling *alone.*

The devil's in the woman for tyranny-----mothers,
wives, mistresses, or sisters, they always will govern
us.—As to my sister Heidelberg, she knows the
strength of her purse, and domineers upon the credit
of it.—" I will do this"—and " you shall do that"
—and " you shall do t'other, or else the fammaly
sha'n't have a farden of"—[*mimicking.*]—So absolute
with her money!—but to say the truth, nothing but
money *can* make us absolute, and so we must e'en
make the best of her.

SCENE *changes to the garden.*

Enter Lord Ogleby, *and* Canton.

Lord Ogle. What! Mademoiselle Fanny to be sent
away!—Why?—Wherefore?—What's the meaning
of all this?

Cant. Je ne scais pas.—I know noting of it.

Lord Ogle. It can't be; it sha'n't be. I protest
against the measure. She's a fine girl, and I had much
rather that the rest of the family were annihilated
than

than that she should leave us.—Her vulgar father, that's the very abstract of 'Change-Alley—the aunt, that's always endeavouring to be a fine lady—and the pert sister, for ever shewing that she is one, are horrid company indeed, and without her would be intolerable. Ah, la petite Fanchon! she's the thing. Is n't she, Cant.?

Cant. Dere is very good sympatie entre vous, and dat young lady, mi Lor.

Lord Ogle. I'll not be left among these Goths and Vandals, your Sterlings, your Heidelbergs, and Devilbergs—if she goes, I'll positively go too.

Cant. In de same post-chay, my Lor? You have no object to dat I believe, nor Mademoiselle neider too—ha! ha! ha!

Lord Ogle. Prithee hold thy foolish tongue, Cant. Does thy Swifs stupidity imagine that I can see and talk with a fine girl without desires?—My eyes are involuntarily attracted by beautiful objects—I fly as naturally to a fine girl—

Cant. As de fine girl to you, my Lor, ha! ha! ha! you alway fly togedre like un pair de pigeons,—

Lord Ogle. Like un pair de pigeons—[*mocks him.*] —Vous etes un fot, Monf. Canton—Thou art always dreaming of my intrigues, and never seeft me *badiner,* but you suspect mischief, you old fool, you.

Cant. I am fool, I confess, but not always fool in dat, my Lor, he! he! he!

Lord Ogle. He! he! he!---Thou art incorrigible, but thy absurdities amuse one.---Thou art like my rappee here, [*takes out his box.*] a most ridiculous superfluity, but a pinch of thee now and then is a more delicious treat.

Cant. You do me great honeur, mi Lor.

Lord Ogle. 'Tis fact, upon my foul.---Thou art properly my cephalic snuff, and art no bad medicine against megrims, vertigoes, and profound thinking--- ha! ha! ha!

Cant.

Cant. Your flatterie, my Lor, vil make me too prode.

Lord Ogle. The girl has some little partiality for me, to be sure: but prithee, Cant, is not that Miss Fanny yonder?

Cant. [*Looking with a glass.*] En verité, 'tis she, my Lor --- 'tis one of de pigeons, --- de pigeons d'amour.

Lord Ogle. Don't be ridiculous, you old monkey,
[*smiling.*

Cant. I am monkeè, I am ole, but I have eye, I have ear, and a little understand, now and den,---

Lord Ogle. Taisez vous bête!

Cant. Elle vous attend, my Lor.---She vil make a love to you.

Lord Ogle. Will she? Have at her then! A fine girl can't oblige me more.---Egad, I find myself a little enjoué---come along, Cant.! she is but in the next walk---but there is such a deal of this damned crinkum-crankum, as Sterling calls it, that one sees people for half an hour before one can get to them---Allons, Monf. Canton, allons donc!
[*Exeunt singing in French.*

Another part of the garden.
Lovewell, *and* Fanny.

Lovew. My dear Fanny, I cannot bear your distress! it overcomes all my resolutions, and I am prepared for the discovery.

Fanny. But how can it be effected before my departure?

Lovew. I'll tell you.---Lord Ogleby seems to entertain a visible partiality for you; and notwithstanding the peculiarities of his behaviour, I am sure that he is humane at the bottom. He is vain to an excess; but withall extremely good-natured, and would do any thing to recommend himself to a lady.---Do you open the whole affair of our marriage to him immediately. It will come with more irresistible persuasion
from

from you than from myself; and I doubt not but you'll gain his friendship and protection at once.--- His influence and authority will put an end to Sir John's solicitations, remove your aunt's and sister's unkindness and suspicions, and, I hope, reconcile your father and the whole family to our marriage.

Fanny. Heaven grant it! Where is my Lord?

Lovew. I have heard him and Canton since dinner singing French songs under the great walnut-tree by the parlour door. If you meet with him in the garden, you may disclose the whole immediately.

Fanny. Dreadful as the task is, I'll do it.---Any thing is better than this continual anxiety.

Lovew. By that time the discovery is made, I will appear to second you.---Ha! here comes my Lord.--- Now, my dear Fanny, summon up all your spirits, plead our cause powerfully, and be sure of success.---

[*going.*

Fanny. Ah, don't leave me!

Lovew. Nay, you must let me.

Fanny. Well, since it must be so, I'll obey you, if I have the power. Oh, Lovewell!

Lovew. Consider, our situation is very critical. To-morrow morning is fixt for your departure, and if we lose this opportunity, we may wish in vain for another.--- He approaches---I must retire.---Speak, my dear Fanny, speak, and make us happy!

[*Exit.*

Fanny *alone.*

Good heaven, what a situation am I in! what shall I do? what shall I say to him? I am all confusion.

Enter Lord Ogleby, *and* Canton.

Lord Ogle. To see so much beauty so solitary, Madam, is a satire upon mankind, and 'tis fortunate that one man has broke in upon your reverie for the credit of our sex.---I say *one,* Madam, for poor

Canton

Canton here, from age and infirmities, ftands for nothing.

Cant. Noting at all, inteed.

Fanny. Your Lordfhip does me great honour.---I had a favour to requeft, my Lord!

Lord Ogle. A favour, Madam!---To be honoured with your commands, is an inexprefiible favour done to me, Madam.

Fanny. If your Lordfhip could indulge me with the honour of a moment's---What is the matter with me?   [*afide.*

Lord Ogle. The girl's confufed---he!---here's fome-thing in the wind, faith---I'll have a tete-a-tete with her---allez vous en!   [*to Canton.*

Cant. I go---ah, pauvre Mademoifelle! my Lor, have *pitié* upon the poor *pigeone!*

Lord Ogle. I'll knock you down, Cant. if you're impertinent.   [*fmiling.*

Cant. Den I mus avay--- [*fhuffles along.*]---You are mofh pleafe, for all dat.   [*afide, and exit.*

Fanny. I fhall fink with apprehenfion.   [*afide.*

Lord Ogle. What a fweet girl!---fhe's a civiliz'd being, and atones for the barbarifm of the reft of the family.

Fanny. My Lord! I--- [*fhe curtfeys, and blufhes.*

Lord Ogle. [*addreffing her.*] I look upon it, Madam, to be one of the luckieft circumftances of my life, that I have this moment the honour of receiving your commands, and the fatisfaction of confirming with my tongue, what my eyes perhaps have but too weakly expreffed---that I am literally---the humbleft of your fervants.

Fanny. I think myfelf greatly honoured, by your Lordfhip's partiality to me; but it diftreffes me, that I am obliged in my prefent fituation to apply to it for protection.

Lord Ogle. I am happy in your diftrefs, Madam, becaufe it gives me an opportunity to fhew my zeal. Beauty to me is a religion, in which I was born and

bred

bred a bigot, and would die a martyr.---I'm in tolerable spirits, faith!   [*aside.*

Fanny. There is not perhaps at this moment a
more distressed creature than myself. Affection,
duty, hope, despair, and a thousand different senti-
ments, are struggling in my bosom; and even the
presence of your Lordship, to whom I have flown for
protection, adds to my perplexity.

Lord Ogle. Does it, Madam?---Venus forbid!---My
old fault; the devil's in me, I think, for perplexing
young women. [*aside, and smiling.*] Take courage,
Madam! dear Miss Fanny, explain.---You have a
powerful advocate in my breast, I assure you---My
heart, Madam---I am attached to you by all the
laws of sympathy, and delicacy.---By my honour,
I am.

Fanny. Then I will venture to unburthen my
mind --- Sir John Melvil, my Lord, by the most
misplaced, and mistimed declaration of affection for
me, has made me the unhappiest of women.

Lord Ogle. How, Madam! Has Sir John made
his addresses to you?

Fanny. He has, my Lord, in the strongest terms.
But I hope it is needless to say, that my duty to my
family, love to my sister, and regard to the whole
family, as well as the great respect I entertain for
your Lordship [*curtseying*] made me shudder at his
addresses.

Lord Ogle. Charming girl!---Proceed, my dear Miss
Fanny, proceed!

Fanny. In a moment---give me leave, my Lord!---
But if what I have to disclose should be received with
anger or displeasure---

Lord Ogle. Impossible, by all the tender powers!---
Speak, I beseech you, or I shall divine the cause
before you utter it.

Fanny. Then, my Lord, Sir John's addresses are
not only shocking to me in themselves, but are more
particularly

particularly difagreeable to me at this time---as---as
[hefitating.

Lord Ogle. As what, Madam?

Fanny. As---pardon my confufion---I am entirely devoted to another.

Lord Ogle. If this is not plain, the devil's in it--- [*afide.*] But tell me, my dear Mifs Fanny, for I muft know; tell me the how, the when, and the where--- Tell me---

Enter Canton haftily.

Cant. My Lor, my Lor, my Lor!

Lord Ogle. Damn your Swifs Impertinence! how durft you interrupt me in the moft critical melting moment that ever love and beauty honoured me with?

Cant. I demande pardonne, my Lor! Sir John Melvil, my Lor, fent me to beg you do him de honeur to fpeak a little to your Lordfhip.

Lord Ogle. I'm not at leifure---I'm bufy---Get away, you ftupid old dog, you Swifs rafcal, or I'll---

Cant. Fort bien, my Lor. [*Cant. goes out on tiptoe.*

Lord Ogle. By the laws of gallantry, Madam, this interruption fhould be death; but as no punifhment ought to difturb the triumph of the fofter paffions, the criminal is pardoned and difmiffed---Let us return, Madam, to the higheft luxury of exalted minds---a declaration of love from the lips of beauty.

Fanny. The entrance of a third perfon has a little relieved me, but I cannot go through with it---and yet I muft open my heart with a difcovery, or it will break with its burthen.

Lord Ogle. What paffion in her eyes! I am alarmed to agitation. [*afide.*] I prefume, Madam, (and as you have flattered me, by making me a party concerned, I hope you'll excufe the prefumption) that---

Fanny. Do you excufe my making you a party concerned, my Lord, and let me intereft your heart in my behalf, as my future happinefs or mifery in a great meafure depend——

Lord

Lord Ogle. Upon me, Madam?

Fanny. Upon you, my Lord.   [*sighs.*

Lord Ogle. There's no ſtanding this: I have caught the infection---her tenderneſs diſſolves me.   [*ſighs.*

Fanny. And ſhould you too ſeverely judge of a raſh action which paſſion prompted, and modeſty has long concealed---

Lord Ogle. [*taking her hand.*] Thou amiable creature---command my heart, for it is vanquiſhed---Speak but thy virtuous wiſhes, and enjoy them.

Fanny. I cannot, my Lord---indeed, I cannot---Mr. Lovewell muſt tell you my diſtreſſes---and when you know them---pity and protect me. --- [*Exit in tears.*

Lord Ogleby *alone.*

How the devil could I bring her to this? It is too much---too much---I can't bear it---I muſt give way to this amiable weakneſs---[*wipes his eyes.*] My heart overflows with ſympathy, and I feel every tenderneſs, I have inſpired---[*ſtifles the tear.*] How blind have I been to the deſolation I have made!---How could I poſſibly imagine that a little partial attention and tender civilities to this young creature ſhould have gathered to this burſt of paſſion! Can I be a man and withſtand it? No---I'll ſacrifice the whole ſex to her. ---But here comes the father, quite *apropos.* I'll open the matter immediately, ſettle the buſineſs with him, and take the ſweet girl down to Ogleby-houſe to-morrow morning---But what the devil! Miſs Sterling too! What miſchief's in the wind now?

Enter Sterling, *and Miſs* Sterling.

Sterl. My Lord, your ſervant! I am attending my daughter here upon rather a diſagreeable affair. Speak to his Lordſhip, Betſey!

Lord Ogle. Your eyes, Miſs Sterling---for I always read the eyes of a young lady---betray ſome little emotion---What are your commands, Madam?

Miſs

Miss Sterl. I have but too much cause for my emotion, my Lord!

Lord Ogle. I cannot commend my kinsman's behaviour, Madam. He has behaved like a false knight, I must confess. I have heard of his apostasy. Miss Fanny has informed me of it.

Miss Sterl. Miss Fanny's baseness has been the cause of Sir John's inconstancy.

Lord Ogle. Nay, now, my dear Miss Sterling, your passion transports you too far. Sir John may have entertained a passion for Miss Fanny, but believe me, my dear Miss Sterling, believe me, Miss Fanny has no passion for Sir John. She has a passion, indeed, a most tender passion. She has opened her whole soul to me, and I know where her affections are placed.
[*conceitedly.*

Miss Sterl. Not upon Mr. Lovewell, my Lord; for I have great reason to think that her seeming attachment to him, is, by his consent, made use of as a blind to cover her designs upon Sir John.

Lord Ogle. Lovewell! No, poor lad! She does not think of him.   [*smiling.*

Miss Sterl. Have a care, my Lord, that both the families are not made the dupes of Sir John's artifice and my sister's dissimulation! You don't know her---indeed, my Lord, you don't know her---a base, insinuating, perfidious!---It is too much---She has been beforehand with me, I perceive. Such unnatural behaviour to me!---But since I see I can have no redress, I am resolved that some way or other I will have revenge.   [*Exit.*

Sterl. This is foolish work, my Lord!

Lord Ogle. I have too much sensibility to bear the tears of beauty.

Sterl. It is touching indeed, my Lord---and very moving for a father.

Lord Ogle. To be sure, Sir!---You must be distrest beyond measure!---Wherefore, to divert your too

F   exquisite

exquifite feeling, fuppofe we change the fubject, and proceed to bufinefs.

Sterl. With all my heart, my Lord!

Lord Ogle. You fee, Mr. Sterling, we can make no union in our families by the propos'd marriage.

Sterl. And very forry I am to fee it, my Lord.

Lord Ogle. Have you fet your heart upon being allied to our houfe, Mr. Sterling?

Sterl. 'Tis my only wifh, at prefent, my omnium, as I may call it.

Lord Ogle. Your wifhes fhall be fulfill'd.

Sterl. Shall they, my Lord!---but how---how?

Lord Ogle. I'll marry in your family.

Sterl. What! my fifter Heidelberg?

Lord Ogle. You throw me into a cold fweat, Mr. Sterling. No, not your fifter---but your daughter.

Sterl. My daughter!

Lord Ogle. Fanny!---now the murder's out!

Sterl. What *you*, my Lord?---

Lord Ogle. Yes---I, I, Mr. Sterling!

Sterl. No, no, my Lord---that's too much. [*fmiling.*

Lord Ogle. Too much?---I don't comprehend you.

Sterl. What, you, my Lord, marry my Fanny!— Blefs me, what will the folks fay?

Lord Ogle. Why, what will they fay?

Sterl. That you're a bold man, my Lord—that's all.

Lord Ogle. Mr. Sterling, this may be city wit for aught I know—Do you court my alliance?

Sterl. To be fure, my Lord.

Lord Ogle. Then I'll explain.—My nephew won't marry your eldeft daughter—nor I neither—Your youngeft daughter won't marry him—I will marry your youngeft daughter.

Sterl. What! with a youngeft daughter's fortune, my Lord?

Lord Ogle. With any fortune, or no fortune at all, Sir. Love is the idol of my heart, and the dæmon Intereft finks before him. So, Sir, as I faid before,

I will

I will marry your youngeſt daughter; your youngeſt daughter will marry me.—

Sterl. Who told you ſo, my Lord?

Lord Ogle. Her own ſweet ſelf, Sir.

Sterl. Indeed?

Lord Ogle. Yes, Sir; our affection is mutual; your advantage double and treble—your daughter will be a Counteſs directly—I ſhall be the happieſt of beings— and you'll be father to an Earl inſtead of a Baronet.

Sterl. But what will my ſiſter ſay?—and my daughter?

Lord Ogle. I'll manage that matter—, nay, if they won't conſent, I'll run away with your daughter in ſpite of you.

Sterl. Well ſaid, my Lord!—your ſpirit's good— I wiſh you had my conſtitution!—but if you'll venture, I have no objection, if my ſiſter has none.

Lord Ogle. I'll anſwer for your ſiſter, Sir. Apropos! the lawyers are in the houſe—I'll have articles drawn, and the whole affair concluded to-morrow morning.

Sterl. Very well: and I'll diſpatch Lovewell to London immediately for ſome freſh papers I ſhall want, and I ſhall leave you to manage matters with my ſiſter. You muſt excuſe me, my Lord, but I can't help laughing at the match—He! he! he! what will the folks ſay? [*Exit.*

Lord Ogle. What a fellow am I going to make a father of?—He has no more feeling than the poſt in his warehouſe—But Fanny's virtues tune me to rapture again, and I won't think of the reſt of the family.

Enter Lovewell *haſtily.*

Lovew. I beg your Lordſhip's pardon, my Lord; are you alone, my Lord?

Lord Ogle. No, my Lord, I am not alone! I am in company, the beſt company.

Lovew. My Lord!

F 2　　　　　　　*Lord*

Lord Ogle. I never was in such exquisite enchanting company since my heart first conceived, or my senses tasted pleasure.

Lovew. Where are they, my Lord ? [*looking about.*

Lord Ogle. In my mind, Sir.

Lovew. What company have you there, my Lord ?
[*smiling.*

Lord Ogle. My own ideas, Sir, which so croud upon my imagination, and kindle it to such a delirium of extasy, that wit, wine, music, poetry, all combined, and each perfection, are but mere mortal shadows of my felicity.

Lovew. I see that your Lordship is happy, and I rejoice at it.

Lord Ogle. You *shall* rejoice at it, Sir ; my felicity shall not selfishly be confined, but shall spread its influence to the whole circle of my friends. I need not say, Lovewell, that you shall have your share of it.

Lovew. Shall I, my Lord ?—then I understand you —you have heard—Miss Fanny has informed you—

Lord Ogle. She has—I have heard, and she shall be happy—'tis determin'd.

Lovew. Then I have reached the summit of my wishes—And will your Lordship pardon the folly ?

Lord Ogle. O yes, poor creature, how could she help it? —'Twas unavoidable—Fate and necessity.

Lovew. It was indeed, my Lord—Your kindness distracts me.

Lord Ogle. And so it did the poor girl, faith.

Lovew. She trembled to disclose the secret, and declare her affections ?

Lord Ogle. The world, I believe, will not think her affections ill placed.

Lovew. [*bowing.*]—You are too good, my Lord. —And do you really excuse the rashness of the action ?

Lord Ogle. From my very soul, Lovewell.

Lovew. Your generosity overpowers me.--[*bowing.*] —I was afraid of her meeting with a cold reception.

Lord

Lord Ogle. More fool you then.

Who pleads her caufe with never-failing beauty,
Here finds a full redrefs.   [*ftrikes his breaft.*
She's a fine girl, Lovewell.

Lovew. Her beauty, my Lord, is her leaft merit.
She has an underftanding——

Lord Ogle. Her choice convinces me of that.

Lovew.—[*bowing.*]—That's your Lordfhip's goodnefs. Her choice was a difinterefted one.

Lord Ogle. No—no—not altogether—it began
with intereft, and ended in paffion.

Lovew. Indeed, my Lord, if you were acquainted
with her goodnefs of heart, and generofity of mind,
as well as you are with the inferior beauties of her
face and perfon——

Lord Ogle. I am fo perfectly convinced of their
exiftence, and fo totally of your mind touching
every amiable particular of that fweet girl, that were
it not for the cold unfeeling impediments of the law,
I would marry her to-morrow morning.

Lovew. My Lord!

Lord Ogle. I would, by all that's honourable in
man, and amiable in woman.

Lovew. Marry her!—Who do you mean, my
Lord?

Lord Ogle. Mifs Fanny Sterling, that is—the Coun-
tefs of Ogleby that fhall be.

Lovew. I am aftonifhed.

Lord Ogle. Why, could you expect lefs from me?

Lovew. I did not expect this, my Lord.

Lord Ogle. Trade and accounts have deftroyed
your feeling.

 · *Lovew.* No, indeed, my Lord.   [*fighs.*

Lord Ogle. The moment that love and pity en-
tered my breaft, I was refolved to plunge into matrimony, and fhorten the girl's tortures—I never do any
thing by halves; do I, Lovewell?

Lovew. No, indeed, my Lord—[*fighs.*]—What
an accident !

Lord Ogle. What's the matter, Lovewell? thou seem'ft to have loft thy faculties. Why don't you wifh me joy, man?

Lovew. O, I do, my Lord. [*fighs.*

Lord Ogle. She faid, that you would explain what fhe had not power to utter—but I wanted no inter-preter for the language of love.

Lovew. But has your Lordfhip confidered the confequences of your refolution?

Lord Ogle. No, Sir, I am above confideration, when my defires are kindled.

Lovew. But confider the confequences, my Lord, to your nephew, Sir John.

Lord Ogle. Sir John has confidered no confequences himfelf, Mr. Lovewell.

Lovew. Mr. Sterling, my Lord, will certainly re-fufe his daughter to Sir John.

Lord Ogle. Sir John has already refufed Mr. Ster-ling's daughter.

Lovew. But what will become of Mifs Sterling, my Lord?

Lord Ogle. What's that to you?—You may have her, if you will.—I depend upon Mr. Sterling's city-philofophy, to be reconciled to Lord Ogleby's being his fon-in-law, inftead of Sir John Melvil, Baronet. Don't you think that your mafter may be brought to that, without having recourfe to his calculations? Eh, Lovewell!

Lovew. But, my Lord, that is not the queftion.

Lord Ogle. Whatever is the queftion, I'll tell you my anfwer.—I am in love with a fine girl, whom I refolve to marry.

Enter Sir John Melvil.

What news with you, Sir John?—You look all hurry and impatience—like a meffenger after a battle.

Sir John. After a battle, indeed, my Lord.—I have this day had a fevere engagement, and wanting your Lordfhip as an auxiliary, I have at laft muftered up

refolution

refolution to declare, what my duty to you and to myfelf have demanded from me fome time.

Lord Ogle. To the bufinefs then, and be as concife as poffible; for I am upon the wing—eh, Lovewell?
                              [*he fmiles, and* Lovewell *bows.*

Sir John. I find 'tis in vain, my Lord, to ftruggle againft the force of inclination.

Lord Ogle. Very true, Nephew, I am your witnefs, and will fecond the motion—fhan't I Lovewell?   [*fmiles, and* Lovewell *bows.*

Sir John. Your Lordfhip's generofity encourages me to tell you—that I cannot marry Mifs Sterling.

Lord Ogle. I am not at all furpriz'd at it—fhe's a bitter potion, that's the truth of it; but as you were to fwallow it, and not I, it was your bufinefs, and not mine—Any thing more?

Sir John. But this, my Lord—that I may be permitted to make my addreffes to the other fifter.

Lord Ogle. O yes—by all means—have you any hopes there, Nephew?—Do you think he'll fucceed, Lovewell?   [*fmiles, and winks at* Lovewell.

Lovew. I think not, my Lord.   [*gravely.*

Lord Ogle. I think fo too; but let the fool try.

Sir John. Will your Lordfhip favour me with your good offices to remove the chief obftacle to the match, the repugnance of Mrs. Heidelberg?

Lord Ogle. Mrs. Heidelberg!—Had not you better begin with the young lady firft? it will fave you a great deal of trouble; won't it, Lovewell?—[*fmiles.*]
—but do what you pleafe, it will be the fame thing to me—won't it, Lovewell?—[*conceitedly.*]—Why don't you laugh at him?

Lovew. I do, my Lord.   [*forces a fmile.*

Sir John. And your Lordfhip will endeavour to prevail on Mrs. Heidelberg to confent to my marriage with Mifs Fanny?

Lord Ogle. I'll fpeak to Mrs. Heidelberg, about the adorable Fanny, as foon as poffible.

Sir John. Your generosity transports me.

Lord Ogle. Poor fellow, what a dupe! he little thinks who's in possession of the town.   [*aside.*

Sir John. And your Lordship is not offended at this seeming inconstancy?

Lord Ogle. Not in the least. Miss Fanny's charms will even excuse infidelity---I look upon women as the *feræ naturæ,*---lawful game---and every man who is qualified, has a natural right to pursue them; Lovewell as well as you, and I as well as either of you.--- Every man shall do his best, without offence to any ---what say you, kinsmen?

Sir John. You have made me happy, my Lord.

Lovew. And me, I assure you, my Lord.

Lord Ogle. And I am superlatively so---*allons donc* ---to horse and away, boys!---you to your affairs, and I to mine---suivons l'amour.   [*sings.*

[*Exeunt severally.*

ACT V. SCENE I.

Fanny's *apartment.*

Enter Lovewell *and* Fanny---*followed by* Betty.

Fanny. WHY did you come so soon, Mr. Lovewell? the family is not yet in bed, and Betty certainly heard somebody listening near the chamber-door.

Betty. My mistress is right, Sir! evil spirits are abroad; and I am sure you are both too good, not to expect mischief from them.

Lovew. But who can be so curious, or so wicked?

Betty. I think we have wickedness and curiosity enough in this family, Sir, to expect the worst.

Fanny. I do expect the worst.---Prithee, Betty, return to the outward door, and listen if you hear

any

any body in the gallery; and let us know directly.

Betty. I warrant you, Madam—the Lord blefs you
both!   [*Exit.*

Fanny. What did my father want with you this
evening?

Lovew. He gave me the key of his clofet, with
orders to bring from London fome papers relating
to Lord Ogleby.

Fanny. And why did not you obey him?

Lovew. Becaufe I am certain that his Lordfhip
has open'd his heart to him about you, and thofe
papers are wanted merely on that account—but as
we fhall difcover all to-morrow, there will be no occafion for them, and it would be idle in me to go.

Fanny. Hark!—hark! blefs me, how I tremble!—
I feel the terrors of guilt—indeed, Mr. Lovewell,
this is too much for me.

Lovew. And for me too, my fweet Fanny. Your
apprehenfions make a coward of me.—But what can
alarm you? your aunt and fifter are in their cham-
bers, and you have nothing to fear from the reft of
the family.

Fanny. I fear every body, and every thing, and
every moment—My mind is in continual agitation
and dread;—indeed, Mr. Lovewell, this fituation
may have very unhappy confequences.   [*weeps.*

Lovew. But it fhan't—I would rather tell our
ftory this moment to all the houfe, and run the
rifque of maintaining you by the hardeft labour,
than fuffer you to remain in this dangerous perplexity.—What! fhall I facrifice all my beft hopes
and affections, in your dear health and fafety, for the
mean, and in fuch a cafe, the meaneft confideration
—of our fortune! Were we to be abandon'd by all
our relations, we have that in our hearts and minds,
will weigh againft the moft affluent circumftances.—
I fhould not have propos'd the fecrecy of our marriage, but for your fake; and with hopes that the
                                                  moft

moſt generous ſacrifice you have made to love and me, might be leſs injurious to you, by waiting a lucky moment of reconciliation.

Fanny. Huſh! huſh! for heav'n ſake, my dear Lovewell, don't be ſo warm!—your generoſity gets the better of your prudence; you will be heard, and we ſhall be diſcovered.—I am ſatisfied, indeed I am. —Excuſe this weakneſs, this delicacy—this what you will.—My mind's at peace—indeed it is—think no more of it, if you love me!

Lovew. That one word has charm'd me, as it always does, to the moſt implicit obedience; it would be the worſt of ingratitude in me to diſtreſs you a moment.   [*kiſſes her.*

 Re-enter Betty.

Betty. [*in a low voice.*] I'm ſorry to diſturb you,

Fanny. Ha! what's the matter?

Lovew. Have you heard any body?

Betty. Yes, yes, I have, and they have heard *you* too, or I am miſtaken—if they had *ſeen* you too, we ſhould have been in a fine quandary.

Fanny. Prithee don't prate now, Betty!

Lovew. What did you hear?

Betty. I was preparing myſelf, as uſual, to take me a little nap.

Lovew. A nap!

Betty. Yes, Sir, a nap; for I watch much better ſo than wide awake; and when I had wrap'd this handkerchief round my head, for fear of the ear-ach from the key-hole, I thought I heard a kind of a ſort of a buzzing, which I firſt took for a gnat, and ſhook my head two or three times, and went ſo with my hand—

Fanny. Well—well—and ſo—

Betty. And ſo, Madam, when I heard Mr. Love-well a little loud, I heard the buzzing louder too—and pulling off my handkerchief ſoftly—I could hear this ſort of noiſe—[*makes an indiſtinct noiſe like ſpeaking.*

Fanny. Well, and what did they ſay?

            Betty.

Betty. Oh! I could not underſtand a word of what was ſaid.

Lovew. The outward door is lock'd?

Betty. Yes; and I bolted it too, for fear of the worſt.

Fanny. Why did you? they muſt have heard you, if they were near.

Betty. And I did it on purpoſe, Madam, and cough'd a little too, that they might not hear Mr. Lovewell's voice—when I was ſilent, they were ſilent, and ſo I came to tell you.

Fanny. What ſhall we do?

Lovew. Fear nothing; we know the worſt; it will only bring on our cataſtrophe a little too ſoon—but Betty might fancy this noiſe—ſhe's in the conſpiracy, and can make a man of a mouſe at any time.

Betty. I can diſtinguiſh a man from a mouſe, as well as my betters—I'm ſorry you think ſo ill of me, Sir.

Fanny. He compliments you, don't be a fool!— Now you have ſet her tongue a running, ſhe'll mutter for an hour. [*to* Lovewell.] I'll go and hearken myſelf. [*Exit.*

Betty. I'll turn my back upon no girl, for ſincerity and ſervice. [*half aſide, and muttering.*

Lovew. Thou art the firſt in the world for both; and I will reward you ſoon, Betty, for one and the other.

Betty. I'm not marcenary neither—I can live on a little, with a good *carreter.*

Re-enter Fanny.

Fanny. All ſeems quiet—ſuppoſe, my dear, you go to your own room—I ſhall be much eaſier then— and to-morrow we will be prepared for the diſcovery.

Betty. You may diſcover, if you pleaſe; but, for my part, I ſhall ſtill be ſecret. [*half aſide, and muttering.*

Lovew. Should I leave you now,—if they ſtill are upon the watch, we ſhall loſe the advantage of our delay.—Beſides, we ſhould conſult upon to-morrow's buſineſs.—Let Betty go to her own room, and lock

the

the outward door after her; we can faſten this; and when ſhe thinks all ſafe, ſhe may return and let me out as uſual.

Betty. Shall I, Madam?

Fanny. Do! let me have my way to-night, and you ſhall command me ever after.—I would not have you ſurprized here for the world.—Pray leave me! I ſhall be quite myſelf again, if you will oblige me.

Lovew. I live only to oblige you, my ſweet Fanny! I'll be gone this moment.   [*going.*

Fanny. Let us liſten firſt at the door, that you may not be intercepted.—Betty ſhall go firſt, and if they lay hold of her——

Betty. They'll have the wrong ſow by the ear, I can tell them that.   [*going haſtily.*

Fanny. Softly—ſoftly—Betty! don't venture out, if you hear a noiſe.—Softly, I beg of you!—See, Mr. Lovewell, the effects of indiſcretion!

Lovew. But love, Fanny, makes amends for all.
      [*Exeunt all ſoftly.*

SCENE *changes to a gallery, which leads to ſeveral bed-chambers.*

Enter Miſs Sterling, *leading Mrs.* Heidelberg *in a night-cap.*

Miſs Sterl. This way, dear Madam, and then I'll tell you all.

Mrs. Heidel. Nay, but Niece—conſider a little—don't drag me out in this figur---let me put on my fly-cap!---if any of my Lord's fammaly, or the counſellors at law, ſhould be ſtirring, I ſhould be perdigus diſconcarted.

Miſs Sterl. But, my dear Madam, a moment is an age, in my ſituation. I am ſure my ſiſter has been plotting my diſgrace and ruin in that chamber---O ſhe's all craft and wickedneſs.

Mrs. Heidel. Well, but ſoftly, Betſey!---you are all in emotion---your mind is too much fluſtrated---you

can

can neither eat nor drink, nor take your natural reft---
compofe yourfelf, child; for if we are not as wary-
fome as they are wicked, we fhall difgrace ourfelves
and the whole fammaly.

Mifs Sterl. We are difgraced already, Madam.---
Sir John Melvil has forfaken me; my Lord cares
for nobody but himfelf; or, if for any body, it is my
fifter; my father, for the fake of a better bargain,
would marry me to a 'Change-broker; fo that if
you, Madam, don't continue my friend---if you forfake me---if I am to lofe my beft hopes and confo-
lation---in your tendernefs---and affec-tions---I had
better---at once---give up the matter---and let my
fifter enjoy---the fruits of her treachery---trample
with fcorn upon the rights of her elder fifter, the
will of the beft of aunts, and the weaknefs of a too
interefted father.

[*fhe pretends to be burfting into tears all this fpeech.*
Mrs. Heidel. Don't, Betfey---keep up your fpurrit---
I hate whimpering---I am your friend---depend upon
me in every partickler---but be compofed, and tell
me what new mifchief you have difcover'd.

Mifs Sterl. I had no defire to fleep, and would not
undrefs myfelf, knowing that my Machiavel fifter
would not reft till fhe had broke my heart:---I was
fo uneafy that I could not ftay in my room, but
when I thought that all the houfe was quiet, I fent
my maid to difcover what was going forward; fhe
immediately came back and told me that they were
in high confultation; that fhe had heard only, for it
was in the dark, my fifter's maid conduct Sir
John Melvil to her miftrefs; and then lock the
door.

Mrs. Heidel. And how did you conduct yourfelf in
this dalimma?

Mifs Sterl. I return'd with her, and could hear a
man's voice, though nothing that they faid diftinctly;
and you may depend upon it, that Sir John is now
in that room, that they have fettled the matter, and
will

will run away together before morning, if we don't prevent them.

Mrs. Heidel. Why the brazen flut! has she got her sister's husband (that is to be) lock'd up in her chamber! at night too!---I tremble at the thoughts!

Miss Sterl. Hush, Madam! I hear something.

Mrs. Heidel. You frighten me---let me put on my fly-cap---I would not be seen in this figur for the world.

Miss Sterl. 'Tis dark, Madam; you can't be seen.

Mrs. Heidel. I protest there's a candle coming, and a man too!

Miss Sterl. Nothing but servants; let us retire a moment! [*they retire.*

Enter Brush *half drunk, laying hold of the* Chamber-maid, *who has a candle in her hand.*

Ch. Maid. Be quiet, Mr. Brush; I shall drop down with terror!

Brush. But my sweet, and most amiable chamber-maid, if you have no love, you may hearken to a little reason; that cannot possibly do your virtue any harm.

Ch. Maid. But you will do me harm, Mr. Brush, and a great deal of harm too—pray let me go—I am ruin'd if they hear you—I tremble like an asp.

Brush. But they shan't hear us—and if you have a mind to be ruined, it shall be the making of your fortune, you little flut, you!—therefore I say it again, if you have no love, hear a little reason!

Ch. Maid. I wonder at your impurence, Mr. Brush, to use me in this manner; this is not the way to keep me company, I assure you.—You are a town rake I see, and now you are a little in liquor, you fear nothing.

Brush. Nothing, by heav'ns, but your frowns, most amiable chamber-maid; I am a little electrified, that's the truth on't; I am not used to drink Port, and

your

your master's is so heady, that a pint of it oversets a claret-drinker.

Ch. Maid. Don't be rude! bless me!—I shall be ruin'd—what will become of me?

Brush. I'll take care of you, by all that's honourable.

Ch. Maid. You are a base man to use me so—I'll cry out, if you don't let me go.—That is Miss Sterling's chamber, that Miss Fanny's, and that Madam Heidelberg's.   [*pointing.*

Brush. And that my Lord Ogleby's, and that my Lady what d'ye call 'em: I don't mind such folks when I'm sober, much less when I am whimsical—rather above that too.

Ch. Maid. More shame for you, Mr. Brush!—you terrify me—you have no modesty.

Brush. O but I have, my sweet spider-brusher!—for instance, I reverence Miss Fanny—she's a most delicious morsel, and fit for a prince—with all my horrors of matrimony, I could marry her myself—but for her sister——

Miss Sterl. There, there, Madam, all in a story!

Ch. Maid. Bless me, Mr. Brush!—I heard something!

Brush. Rats, I suppose, that are gnawing the old timbers of this execrable old dungeon—If it was mine, I would pull it down, and fill your fine canal up with the rubbish; and then I should get rid of two damn'd things at once.

Ch. Maid. Law! law! how you blaspheme!—we shall have the house upon our heads for it.

Brush. No, no, it will last our time—but as I was saying, the elder sister—Miss Jezabel——

Ch. Maid. Is a fine young lady, for all your evil tongue.

Brush. No—we have smoak'd her already; and unless she marries our old Swiss, she can have none of us—no, no, she won't do—we are a little too nice.

2

        Ch. Maid.

Ch. Maid. You're a monstrous rake, Mr. Brush, and don't care what you say.

Brush. Why, for that matter, my dear, I am a little inclined to mischief; and if you won't have pity upon me, I will break open that door and ravish Mrs. Heidelberg.

Mrs. Heidel. [*coming forward.*] There's no bearing this—you profligate monster!

Ch. Maid. Ha! I am undone!

Brush. Zounds! here she is, by all that's monstrous. [*runs off.*

Miss Sterl. A fine discourse you have had with that fellow!

Mrs. Heidel. And a fine time of night it is to be here with that drunken monster!

Miss Sterl. What have you to say for yourself?

Ch. Maid. I can say nothing.—I am so frighten'd, and so asham'd—but indeed I am vartuous—I am vartuous indeed.

Mrs. Heidel. Well, well—don't tremble so; but tell us what you know of this horrable plot here.

Miss Sterl. We'll forgive you, if you'll discover all.

Ch. Maid. Why, Madam—don't let me betray my fellow servants—I shan't sleep in my bed, if I do.

Mrs. Heidel. Then you shall sleep somewhere else to-morrow night.

Ch. Maid. O dear!—what shall I do?

Mrs. Heidel. Tell us this moment,—or I'll turn you out of doors directly.

Ch. Maid. Why our butler has been treating us below in his pantry—Mr. Brush forc'd us to make a kind of a holiday night of it.

Miss Sterl. Holiday! for what?

Ch. Maid. Nay I only made one.

Miss Sterl. Well, well; but upon what account?

Ch. Maid. Because, as how, Madam, there was a change in the family they said,—that his honour, Sir John—was to marry Miss Fanny instead of your Ladyship.

Miss

Miſs Sterl. And ſo you made a holiday for that—Very fine!

Ch. Maid. I did not make it, Ma'am.

Mrs. Heidel. But do you know nothing of Sir John's being to run away with Miſs Fanny to-night?

Ch. Maid. No, indeed, Ma'am!

Miſs Sterl. Nor of his being now locked up in my ſiſter's chamber?

Ch. Maid. No, as I hope for marcy, Ma'am.

Mrs. Heidel. Well, I'll put an end to all this directly—do you run to my brother Sterling—

Ch. Maid. Now, Ma'am!—'Tis ſo very late, Ma'am—

Mrs. Heidel. I don't care how late it is. Tell him there are thieves in the houſe—that the houſe is o'fire—tell him to come here immediately—go, I ſay!

Ch. Maid. I will, I will, though I'm frighten'd out of my wits. [*Exit.*

Mrs. Heidel. Do you watch here, my dear; and I'll put myſelf in order, to face them. We'll plot 'em, and counter-plot 'em too. [*Exit into her chamber.*

Miſs Sterl. I have as much pleaſure in this revenge, as in being made a counteſs!—Ha! they are unlocking the door.—Now for it! [*retires.*

Fanny's *door is unlock'd—and* Betty *comes out with a candle.* Miſs Sterling *approaches her.*

Betty. [*calling within.*] Sir, Sir!—now's your time—all's clear. [*Seeing Miſs Sterl.*] Stay, ſtay—not yet—we are watch'd.

Miſs Sterl. And ſo you are, Madam Betty!

[*Miſs* Sterling *lays hold of her, while* Betty *locks the door, and puts the key into her pocket.*

Betty. [*turning round.*] What's the matter, Madam?

Miſs Sterl. Nay, that you ſhall tell my father and aunt, Madam.

Betty. I am no tell-tale, Madam, and no thief; they'll get nothing from me.

Miſs Sterl. You have a great deal of courage,

G   Betty;

Betty; and confidering the fecrets you have to keep, you have occafion for it.

Betty. My miftrefs fhall never repent her good opinion of me, Ma'am.

Enter Sterling.

Sterl. What is all this? what's the matter? why am I difturbed in this manner?

Mifs Sterl. This creature, and my diftreffes, Sir, will explain the matter.

Re-enter Mrs. Heidelberg, *with another head-drefs.*

Mrs. Heidel. Now I'm prepar'd for the rancounter —well, brother, have you heard of this fcene of wickednefs?

Sterl. Not I—but what is it? Speak!—I was got into my little clofet—all the lawyers were in bed, and I had almoft loft my fenfes in the confufion of Lord Ogleby's mortgages, when I was alarmed with a foolifh girl, who could hardly fpeak; and whether it's fire, or thieves, or murder, or a rape, I am quite in the dark.

Mrs. Heidel. No, no, there's no rape, brother!— all parties are willing, I believe.

Mifs Sterl. Who's in that chamber?

[*detaining* Betty, *who feemed to be ftealing away.*

Betty. My miftrefs.

Mifs Sterl. And who is with your miftrefs?

Betty. Why, who fhould there be?

Mifs Sterl. Open the door then, and let us fee!

Betty. The door is open, Madam. [*Mifs* Sterling *goes to the door.*] I'll fooner die than peach!

[*Exit haftily.*

Mifs Sterl. The door's lock'd; and fhe has got the key in her pocket.

Mrs. Heidel. There's impudence, brother! piping hot from your daughter Fanny's fchool!

Sterl. But, zoùnds! what is all this about? You tell me of a fum total, and you don't produce the particulars.

Mrs

4

Mrs. Heidel. Sir John Melvil is lock'd up in your daughter's bed-chamber.---There is the particular!

Sterl. The devil he is?---That's bad!

Miss Sterl. And he has been there some time too.

Sterl. Ditto!

Mrs. Heidel. Ditto! worse and worse, I say. I'll raise the house, and expose him to my Lord, and the whole fammaly.

Sterl. By no means! we shall expose ourselves, sister!---the best way is to insure privately---let me alone!---I'll make him marry her to-morrow morning.

Miss Sterl. Make him marry her! this is beyond all patience!---You have thrown away all your affection; and I shall do as much by my obedience: unnatural fathers make unnatural children.---My revenge is in my own power, and I'll indulge it.---Had they made their escape, I should have been exposed to the derision of the world: but the deriders shall be derided; and so-.-help! help, there! thieves! thieves!

Mrs. Heidel. Tit-for-tat, Betsey! you are right, my girl.

Sterl. Zounds! you'll spoil all---you'll raise the whole family,---the devil's in the girl.

Mrs. Heidel. No, no; the devil's in *you*, brother. I am asham'd of your principles.---What! would you connive at your daughter's being lock'd up with her sister's husband? Help! thieves! thieves! I say.

             [cries out.

Sterl. Sister, I beg you!---daughter, I command you!---If you have no regard for me, consider yourselves!---we shall lose this opportunity of ennobling our blood and getting above twenty *per cent.* for our money.

Miss Sterl. What, by my disgrace and my sister's triumph! I have a spirit above such mean considerations; and to shew you that it is not a low-bred, vulgar 'Change-Alley spirit---help! help! thieves! thieves! thieves! I say.

          Sterl.

Sterl. Ay, ay, you may fave your lungs---the houfe is in an uproar;---women at beft have no difcretion; but in a paffion they'll fire a houfe, or burn themfelves in it, rather than not be revenged.

Enter Canton, *in a night-gown and flippers.*

Cant. Eh, diable! vat is de raifon of dis great noife, dis tintamarre?

Sterl. Afk thofe ladies, Sir; 'tis of their making.

Lord Ogleby [*calls within.*]

Brufh! Brufh!---Canton! where are you?---What's the matter? [*rings a bell.*] Where are you?

Sterl. 'Tis my Lord calls, Mr. Canton.

Cant. I com, mi Lor! --- [*Exit* Canton.]--- [*Lord* Ogleby *still rings.*

Serjeant Flower [*calls within.*]

A light! a light here!---where are the fervants? Bring a light for me and my brothers.

Sterl. Lights here! lights for the gentlemen!

[*Exit* Sterling.

Mrs. Heidel. My brother feels, I fee---your fifter's turn will come next.

Mifs Sterl. Ay, ay, let it go round, Madam, it is the only comfort I have left.

Re-enter Sterling, *with lights, before Serjeant* Flower *(with one boot and a flipper)* and Traverfe.

Sterl. This way, Sir! this way, gentlemen!

Serjeant Flower. Well; but Mr. Sterling, no danger I hope.---Have they made a burglarious entry?--- Are you prepared to repulfe them?---I am very much alarm'd about thieves at circuit-time.---They would be particularly fevere with us gentlemen of the bar.

Traverfe. No danger, Mr. Sterling,---no trefpafs, I hope?

Sterl. None, gentlemen, but of thofe ladies making.

Mrs. Heidel. You'll be afham'd to know, gentlemen, that all your labours and ftudies about this

5   young

young lady are thrown away---Sir John Melvil is at this moment lock'd up with this lady's younger fister.

Serjeant Flower. The thing is a little extraordinary, to be fure---but, why were we to be frighten'd out of our beds for this? Could not we have try'd this caufe to-morrow morning?

Mifs Sterl. But, Sir, by to-morrow morning, per-haps, even your affiftance would not have been of any fervice---the birds now in that cage would have flown away.

Enter Lord Ogleby [*in his robe-de-chambre, night-cap, &c.---leaning on* Canton.]

Lord Ogle. I had rather lofe a limb than my night's reft---what's the matter with you all?

Sterl. Ay, ay, 'tis all over!---Here's my Lord too.

Lord Ogle. What's all this fhrieking and fcream-ing?---Where's my angelick Fanny? She's fafe, I hope!

Mrs. Heidel. Your angelick Fanny, my Lord, is lock'd up with your angelick nephew in that chamber.

Lord Ogle. My nephew! then will I be excommu-nicated.

Mrs. Heidel. Your nephew, my Lord, has been plotting to run away with the younger fifter; and the younger fifter has been plotting to run away with your nephew: and if we had not watch'd them and call'd up the fammaly, they had been upon the fcamper to Scotland by this time.

Lord Ogle. Look'ee, ladies!---I know that Sir John has conceived a violent paffion for Mifs Fanny; and I know too that Mifs Fanny has conceived a violent paffion for another perfon; and I am fo well convinc'd of the rectitude of her affections, that I will fupport them with my fortune, my honour, and my life.---Eh, fhan't I, Mr. Sterling? [*fmiling.*] what fay you?---

Sterl.

Sterl. [*fulkily.*] To be fure, my Lord.---Thefe bawling women have been the ruin of every thing.

[*afide.*

Lord Ogle. But come, I'll end this bufinefs in a trice---if you, ladies, will compofe yourfelves, and Mr. Sterling will infure Mifs Fanny from violence, I will engage to draw her from her pillow with a whifper thro' the keyhole.

Mrs. Heidel. The horrid creatures!---I fay, my Lord, break the door open.

Lord Ogle. Let me beg of your delicacy not to be too precipitate!---Now to our experiment!

[*advancing towards the door.*

Mifs Sterl. Now, what will they do?---my heart will beat through my bofom.

Enter Betty, *with the key.*

Betty. There's no occafion for breaking open doors, my Lord; we have done nothing that we ought to be afham'd of, and my miftrefs fhall face her enemies.---

[*going to unlock the door.*

Mrs. Heidel. There's impudence.

Lord Ogle. The myftery thickens. Lady of the bed-chamber! [*to* Betty.] open the door, and intreat Sir John Melvil (for thefe ladies will have it that he is there) to appear and anfwer to high crimes and mif-demeanors.---Call Sir John Melvil into the court!

Enter Sir John Melvil, *on the other fide.*

Sir John. I am here, my Lord.

Mrs. Heidel. Heyday!

Mifs Sterl. Aftonifhment!

Sir John. What is all this alarm and confufion? there is nothing but hurry in the houfe; what is the reafon of it?

Lord Ogle. Becaufe you have been in that cham-ber; *have* been! nay, you *are* there at this moment, as thefe ladies have protefted, fo don't deny it---

Traverfe. This is the cleareft *alibi* I ever knew, Mr. Serjeant,

Flower.

Flower. Luce clarius.

Lord Ogle. Upon my word, ladies, if you have often these frolicks, it would be really entertaining to pafs a whole fummer with you. But come [*to* Betty.] open the door, and intreat your amiable miftrefs to come forth, and difpel all our doubts with her fmiles.

Betty. [*opening the door.*] Madam, you are wanted in this room.   [*pertly.*

Enter Fanny, *in great confufion.*

Mifs Sterl. You fee fhe's ready dreffed---and what confufion fhe's in!

Mrs. Heidel. Ready to pack of, bag and baggage! ---her guilt confounds her!---

Flower. Silence in the court, ladies!

Fanny. I *am* confounded, indeed, Madam!

Lord Ogle. Don't droop, my beauteous lily! but with your own peculiar modefty declare your ftate of mind.---Pour conviction into their ears and raptures into mine.   [*fmiling.*

Fanny. I am at this moment the moft unhappy--- moft diftreft---the tumult is too much for my heart--- and I want the power to reveal a fecret, which to con- ceal has been the misfortune and mifery of my--- my---   [*faints away.*

Lord Ogle. She faints; help, help! for the fair- eft, and beft of women!

Betty. [*running to her.*] O my dear miftrefs!--- help, help, there!---

Sir John. Ha! let me fly to her affiftance.

[*fpeaking all at once.*

Lovewell *rufhes out from the chamber.*

Lovew. My Fanny in danger! I can contain no longer.---Prudence were now a crime; all other cares were loft in this!---fpeak, fpeak to me, my deareft Fanny!---let me but hear thy voice, open your eyes, and blefs me with the fmalleft fign of life!

[*during this fpeech they are all in amazement.*
Mifs Sterl. Lovewell!---I am eafy.---

Mrs. Heidel. I am thunderſtruck !

Lord Ogle. I am petrify'd !

Sir John. And I undone !

Fanny. [*recovering.*] O Lovewell !---even ſupported by thee, I dare not look my father nor his Lordſhip in the face.

Sterl. What now ! did not I ſend you to London, Sir ?

Lord Ogle. Eh !---What !---How's this ?---by what right and title have you been half the night in that lady's bed-chamber ?

Lovew. By that right which makes me the happieſt of men ; and by a title which I would not forego, for any the beſt of kings could give.

Betty. I could cry my eyes out to hear his magni-mity.

Lord Ogle. I am annihilated !

Sterl. I have been choaked with rage and wonder ; but now I can ſpeak.---Zounds, what have you to ſay to me ?---Lovewell, you are a villain.---You have broke your word with me.

Fanny. Indeed, Sir, he has not---You forbad him to think of me, when it was out of his power to obey you ; we have been married theſe four months.

Sterl. And he ſhan't ſtay in my houſe four hours. What baſeneſs and treachery ! As for you, you ſhall repent this ſtep as long as you live, Madam.

Fanny. Indeed, Sir, it is impoſſible to conceive the tortures I have already endured in conſequence of my diſobedience. My heart has continually upbraid-ed me for it ; and though I was too weak to ſtruggle with affection, I feel that I muſt be miſerable for ever without your forgiveneſs.

Sterl. Lovewell, you ſhall leave my houſe direct-ly ;---and you ſhall follow him, Madam. [*to* Fanny.

Lord Ogle. And if they do, I will receive them into mine. Look ye, Mr. Sterling, there have been ſome

miſtakes,

miftakes, which we had all better forget for our own fakes; and the beft way to forget them is to forgive the caufe of them; which I do from my foul.---Poor girl! I fwore to fupport her affection with my life and fortune;---'tis a debt of honour, and muft be paid--- you fwore as much too, Mr. Sterling; but your laws in the city will excufe *you*, I fuppofe; for you never ftrike a balance without errors excepted.

Sterl. I am a father, my Lord; but for the fake of all other fathers, I think I ought not to forgive her, for fear of encouraging other filly girls like herfelf to throw themfelves away without the confent of their parents.

Lovew. I hope there will be no danger of that, Sir. Young ladies with minds, like my Fanny's, would ftartle at the very fhadow of vice; and when they know to what uneafinefs only an indifcretion has expofed her, her example, inftead of encouraging, will rather ferve to deter them.

Mrs. Heidel. Indifcretion, quoth a! a mighty pretty delicat word to exprefs obedience!

Lord Ogle. For my part, I indulge my own paffions too much to tyrannize over thofe of other people. Poor fouls, I pity them. And you muft forgive them too. Come, come, melt a little of your flint, Mr. Sterling!

Sterl. Why, why---as to that, my Lord---to be fure he is a relation of yours, my Lord---what fay *you*, fifter Heidelberg?

Mrs. Heidel. The girl's ruined, and I forgive her.

Sterl. Well---fo do I then.---Nay, no thanks--- [*to Lovewell and Fanny, who feem preparing to fpeak.*] there's an end of the matter.

Lord Ogle. But Lovewell, what makes you dumb all this while?

Lovew. Your kindnefs, my Lord---I can fcarce believe my own fenfes---they are all in a tumult of fear, joy, love, expectation, and gratitude; I ever was, and am now more bound in duty to your Lordfhip.

ship. For you, Mr. Sterling, if every moment of my life, spent gratefully in your service, will in some measure compensate the want of fortune, you perhaps will not repent your goodness to me. And you, ladies, I flatter myself, will not for the future suspect me of artifice and intrigue---I shall be happy to oblige and serve you.---As for you, Sir John——

Sir John. No apologies to me, Lovewell, I do not deserve any. All I have to offer in excuse for what has happened, is my total ignorance of your situation. Had you dealt a little more openly with me, you would have saved me, and yourself, and that lady, (who I hope will pardon my behaviour) a great deal of uneasiness. Give me leave, however, to assure you, that light and capricious as I may have appeared, now my infatuation is over, I have sensibility enough to be ashamed of the part I have acted, and honour enough to rejoice at your happiness.

Lovew. And now, my dearest Fanny, though we are seemingly the happiest of beings, yet all our joys will be dampt, if his Lordship's generosity and Mr. Sterling's forgiveness should not be succeeded by the indulgence, approbation, and consent of these our best benefactors. [*To the audience.*

F I N I S.

EPILOGUE.

Written by Mr. GARRICK.

CHARACTERS *of the* EPILOGUE.

Lord Minum - - - -	Mr. DODD.
Colonel Trill - - - -	Mr. VERNON.
Sir Patrick Mahony - -	Mr. MOODY.
Miss Crotchet - - - -	Mrs. ————
Mrs. Quaver - - - -	Mrs. LEE.
First Lady - - - -	Mrs. BRADSHAW.
Second Lady - - - -	Miss MILLS.
Third Lady - - - -	Mrs. DORMAN.

SCENE, an Assembly.

Several Persons at Cards, at different Tables; among the rest
Col. Trill, *Lord* Minum, *Mrs.* Quaver, *Sir* Patrick Mahony.

At the Quadrille Table.

Col. T. LADIES, with Leave---
   2d Lady. Pass!
    3d Lady. Pass!
     Mrs. Qu. You must do more.

Col. T. Indeed I can't.
 Mrs. Qu. I play in Hearts.
   Col. T. Encore!

2d Lady. What Luck!
  Col. T. To-night at Drury-Lane is play'd
A Comedy, and *toute nouvelle*---a Spade!
Is not Miss Crotchet at the Play?
   Mrs. Q. My Niece
Has made a Party, Sir, to damn the Piece.

At the Whist Table.

Ld. Min. I hate a Playhouse---Trump!---It makes me sick.
1st Lady. We're two by Honours, Ma'am.
   Ld. Min. And we th' odd Trick.
Pray do you know the Author, Colonel Trill?
Col. T. I know no Poets, Heav'n be prais'd!---Spadille!---
1st Lady. I'll tell you who, my Lord! *[Whispers my Lord.*
   Ld. Min. What, he again?
" And dwell such daring Souls in little Men?"
Be whose it will, they down our Throats will cram it!
Col. T. O, no.---I have a Club---the best.---We'll damn it.
       Mrs.

EPILOGUE.

Mrs. Qu. O bravo, Colonel! Mufic is my Flame.

Ld. Min. And mine, by Jupiter!---We've won the Game.

Col. T. What, do you love all Mufick?

       Mrs. Qu. No, not Handel's,

 And nafty Plays---

    Lord Min. Are fit for Goths and Vandals.

         [Rife from the Table and pay.

    From the Piquette Table.

Sir Pat. Well, faith and troth! that Shakefpeare was no Fool!

Col. T. I'm glad you like him, Sir!---So ends the Pool!

         [Pay and rife from Table.

   SONG *by the Colonel.*

  I hate all their Nonfenfe,
   Their Shakefpeares and Johnfons,
 Their Plays, and their Playhoufe, and Bards;
  'Tis finging, not faying;
  A Fig for all playing,
 But playing, as we do, at Cards!

  I love to fee Jonas,
   Am pleas'd too with Comus;
 Each well the Spectator rewards.
  So clever, fo neat in
  Their Tricks, and their Cheating!
 Like them we would fain deal our Cards.

Sir Pat. King Lare is touching!---And how fine to fee
  Ould Hamlet's Ghoft!---" To be, or not to be."---
  What are your Op'ras to Othello's Roar?
  Oh, he's an Angel of a Blackamoor!

Ld. Min. What, when he choaks his Wife?---

      Col. T. And calls her Whore?

Sir Pat. King Richard calls his Horfe---And then Macbeth,
  Whene'er he murders---takes away the Breath.
  My Blood runs cold at every Syllable,
  To fee the Dagger---that's invifible. *[All laugh.*

Sir Pat. Laugh if you pleafe, a pretty Play---

      Ld. Min. Is pretty.

Sir Pat. And when there's Wit in't---

      Col. T. To be fure 'tis witty.

Sir Pat. I love the Playhoufe now---fo light and gay,
  With all thofe Candles, they have ta'en away!

         [All laugh.

  For all your Game, what makes it fo much brighter?

Col. T. Put out the Lights, and then---

      Ld. Min. 'Tis fo much lighter,

Sir Pat. Pray do you mane, Sirs, more than you exprefs?

Col. T. Juft as it happens---

    Ld. Min. Either more, or lefs,

           Mrs.

EPILOGUE.

Mrs. Qu. An't you afham'd, Sir?   [*To Sir Patrick.*

    Sir Pat. Me!---I feldom blufh:---

For little Shakefpeare, faith! I'd take a Pufh!

Ld. Min. News, News!---here comes Mifs Crotchet from the Play.

    Enter Mifs Crotchet.

Mrs. Qu. Well, Crotchet, what's the News?

       Mifs Cro. We've loft the Day.

Col. T. Tell us, dear Mifs, all you have heard and feen.

Mifs Cro. I'm tir'd---a Chair---here, take my Capuchin!

Ld. Min. And isn't it damn'd, Mifs?

      Mifs Cro. No, my Lord, not quite:

But we fhall damn it.

    Col. T. When?

      Mifs Cro. To-morrow Night.

There is a Party of us, all of Fafhion,

Refolv'd to exterminate this vulgar Paffion:

A Playhoufe, what a Place!---I muft forfwear it.

A little Mifchief only makes one bear it.

Such Crowds of City Folks!---fo rude and preffing!

And their Horfe-Laughs, fo hideoufly diftreffing!

Whene'er we hifs'd, they frown'd and fell a fwearing,

Like their own Guildhall Giants---fierce and ftaring!

Col. T. What faid the Folks of Fafhion? were they crofs?

Ld. Min. The reft have no more Judgment than my Horfe.

Mifs Cro. Lord Grimly fwore 'twas execrable Stuff.

Says one, Why fo, my Lord?---My Lord took Snuff.

In the firft Act Lord George began to doze,

And criticis'd the Author---through his Nofe;

So loud indeed, that as his Lordfhip fnor'd,

The Pit turn'd round, and all the Brutes encor'd.

Some Lords, indeed, approv'd the Author's Jokes.

Ld. Min. We have among us, Mifs, *fome* foolifh Folks.

Mifs Cro. Says poor Lord Simper---Well, now to my Mind

The Piece is good;---but he's both deaf and blind.

Sir Pat. Upon my Soul a very pretty Story!

And Quality appears in all its Glory!---

There was fome Merit in the Piece, no Doubt;

Mifs Cro. O, to be fure!---if one could find it out.

Col. T. But tell us, Mifs, the Subject of the Play.

Mifs Cro. Why, 'twas a Marriage---yes, a Marriage---Stay!

A Lord, an Aunt, two Sifters, and a Merchant---

A Baronet---ten Lawyers---a fat Serjeant---

Are all produc'd---to talk with one another;

And about fomething make a mighty Pother;

They all go in, and out; and to, and fro;

And talk, and quarrel---as they come and go---

Then go to Bed, and then get up---and then---

Scream, faint, fcold, kifs,---and go to Bed again.

          [*All laugh.*

          Such

EPILOGUE.

Such is the Play---Your Judgment! never sham it.

Col. T. Oh, damn it!

   Mrs. Qu. Damn it!

    1st Lady. Damn it!

     Miss Cro. Damn it!

      Ld. Min. Damn it!

Sir Pat. Well, faith, you speak your Minds, and I'll be free --
Good Night! this Company's too good for me. [*Going.*

Col. T. Your Judgment, dear Sir Patrick, makes us proud.
           [*All laugh.*

Sir Pat. Laugh if you please, but pray don't laugh too loud.
            [*Exit.*

RECITATIVE.

Col. T. Now the Barbarian's gone, Miss, tune your Tongue,
And let us raise our Spirits high with Song!

RECITATIVE.

Miss Cro. Colonel, *de tout mon Cœur*---I've one in *petto*,
Which you shall join, and make it a *Duetto.*

RECITATIVE.

Ld. Min. Bella Signora, et Amico mio!
I too will join, and then we'll make a *Trio.*---

Col. T. Come all and join the full-mouth'd Chorus,
And drive all Tragedy and Comedy before us!

All the Company rise, and advance to the Front of the Stage.

AIR.

Col. T. Would you ever go to see a Tragedy?

   Miss Cro. Never, never.

  Col. T. A Comedy?

    Ld. M. Never, never,

     Live for ever!

    Tweedle-dum and Tweedle-dee!

  Col. T. *Lord M.* and *Miss Cro.*

  Live for ever!

    Tweedle-dum and Tweedle-dee!

CHORUS.

Would you ever go to see, &c.

PLAYS and FARCES
Printed for T. BECKET and Co. in the Strand.

TIMANTHES, a Tragedy, price 1s. 6d.
    Man and Wife, a Comedy, 1s. 6d.
The Oxonian in Town, a Farce, 1s.
A Peep behind the Curtain, or the New Rehearsal; the Third
    Edition, 1s.-------The Songs of the Burletta Part may be had
    separate, price 6d.
The Widow'd Wife, a Comedy, 1s. 6d.
The Clandestine Marriage, a Comedy, 1s. 6d.
The English Merchant, a Comedy, 1s. 6d.
Cymon, a Dramatic Romance, 1s. 6d.
The Country Girl, a Comedy, 1s. 6d.
The Jealous Wife, a Comedy, 1s. 6d.
Neck or Nothing, a Farce, 1s.
The Musical Lady, a Farce, 1s.
Polly Honeycomb, a Farce, 1s.
The Deuce is in Him, a Farce, 1s.
The Minor, a Comedy, 1s. 6d.
The Citizen, a Farce, 1s.
The Cunning Man, a Musical Entertainment, 1s.
Thomas and Sally, a Musical Entertainment, 1s.
Daphne and Amintor, a Musical Entertainment, 1s.
Love in a Village, an Opera, 1s. 6d.
Maid of the Mill, an Opera, 1s. 6d.
The Capricious Lovers, an Opera, 1s. 6d.
Ditto, a Farce, 1s.
The Plain Dealer, a Comedy, 1s. 6d.
Almena, an Opera, 1s.
The Shepherd's Artifice, a Pastoral, 1s.
Love at first Sight, a Ballad Farce, 1s.
Cymbeline, by Shakespeare, new Edition, 6d.
King Lear, by Shakespeare, new Edition, 6d.
Macbeth, by Shakespeare, 6d.
All for Love, by Shakespeare, 6d.
The Statesman foil'd, a Musical Comedy, 1s.
The Companion to the Playhouse, containing an Account of all
    Plays and Farces, &c. from the Commencement of the Thea-
    tres to the present Time, and also the Lives of the Writers.
    In Form of a Dictionary, two Volumes, 7s.
Catherine and Petruchio, 1s.
The Farmer's Return, 1s.
Florizel and Perdita, 1s.
The Gamester, 1s.
The Enchanter, 1s.
Isabella, 1s.
Miss in her Teens, 1s.
Theobald's Shakespeare, new Edition, in 8 Vols. 1l. 8s.
Mr. Capell's Edition of Shakespeare, beautifully printed, in
    10 Vols. 2l. 2s.

The

Lightning Source UK Ltd.
Milton Keynes UK
UKHW030635010323
417851UK00008B/331